Kaffe Quilts Again

20 favorite quilts in new colorways from Rowan

featuring **Roberta Horton, Mary Mashuta, Liza Prior Lucy, Pauline Smith, and Brandon Mably**

The Taunton Press

R O W A N

The Taunton Press
Inspiration for hands-on living®

The Taunton Press, Inc., 63 South Main Street,
PO Box 5506, Newtown, CT 06470-5506
email: tp@taunton.com

First published in Great Britain in 2012 by
Rowan
Green Lane Mill
Holmfirth
West Yorkshire
England HD9 2DX

Copyright © Westminster Fibers, Inc. 2012
3430 Toringdon Way, Suite 301
Charlotte, NC 28277
U.S.A

Patchwork designs	Kaffe Fassett, Roberta Horton, Mary Mashuta, Liza Prior Lucy, Pauline Smith, Brandon Mably
Art director/styling	Kaffe Fassett
Front cover design	Alison Wilkes
Editor	Pauline Smith
Technical editor	Ruth Eglinton
Designer	Anne Wilson
Location photography	Debbie Patterson
Still photography	Dave Tolson
Illustrations	Ruth Eglinton
Quilters	Judy Irish, Pauline Smith

Publishing consultant   Susan Berry

Library of Congress Cataloging-in-Publication Data

Fassett, Kaffe.
 Kaffe quilts again : 20 favorite quilts in new colorways
from Rowan.
   p. cm.
 ISBN 978-1-60085-766-9
1. Quilting--Patterns. 2. Patchwork--Patterns. I. Title.
TT835.F3696 2012
746.46--dc23

                              2012005753

Color reproduction and printing by KHL Chroma Graphics
and KHL Printing, Singapore

Contents

introduction

What is it about a traditional, unspoilt working farming village that affects us so deeply? We decided to photograph this book in just such a village in Bulgaria, three hours from Sofia. We were introduced to it by our Bulgarian friend, Chris, and we stayed in a house built by his great-grandfather – Chris's wife Dora grew up around the corner. When we met Chris and Dora in London, we should have guessed from their warmth and generosity of spirit that they came from somewhere special.

The unselfconscious aesthetics that naturally occur in an old farming culture like this one gave us just the right setting for the glowing colours of our quilts. The domestic animals, donkeys, horses, pigs and poultry give a self-sustaining security to the place, but what really caught our eye was the fecund vegetable and fruit crops ripening in the autumn sun on the porches of the village houses, and the patched faded doors and rich rust-coloured tiled roofs. They echoed the colours in our quilts perfectly.

Living there for the days of our shoot we were introduced to their traditions: making their own brandy from the grape arbours on each house, bottling their own preserves and tomatoes and making the feta cheese that is a staple of every meal. The full flavour of those deep red tomatoes and the exquisite white peaches that we plucked warm off the trees is still singing on my palette.

Self-sufficiency can lead over the years to a beautiful way of life and in villages like this not much has changed. The tools and implements used are often hand-made and certainly the structures of the houses and barns have the harmonious beauty of traditional and functional design. The terracotta

roof tiles and the half-timbered wood combines with the soft red adobe bricks to make an organic arrangement that is long-lasting but at the same time offers the richness for the eye that is usually so disastrously lacking in modern towns and cities. We seem to have forgotten for the most part how to create graceful shapes in our houses and office buildings. Maybe the rural materials in villages like this – weathered wood, clay and stone – are difficult to use in an ugly way.

We stayed at our village during especially warm weather in September and we ate nearly all our meals in Chris's family garden, surrounded by peach and birch trees, hedges of ivy, and a screen of brilliant magenta-coloured morning glories. One memorable meal, though, we had in an apple orchard next to a hayloft where the corn was stored and the family donkey tethered, while the chickens clucked around us. It was a visual as well as a real feast. A long table draped in a dark brown cloth made the dishes of plentiful food look really luscious. To the side of the table stretched a field of crisp, silver cabbage plants bordered by an arbour dripping with chandelier-like bunches of grapes. Our water came from the well that each house has – cool and refreshing on the hot days of our visit.

I think this tranquil and unforgettable setting has created a special mood for this particular collection of quilts, and it is wonderful to be able to share what was, for us, a truly golden experience.

finding new colours for old blocks

It is always exciting for me as an artist to revisit a past theme or layout. It is the same deep satisfaction that I get from doing different colourways on my fabric designs. For one thing, I travel the world teaching various quilt layouts and get to see how class after class brings such imagination to my original idea. So I thought it would be an interesting exercise in this book if my team of quilt designers and I put ourselves in the students' shoes, as it were, and revisited some favourite block patterns from past books with the new range of fabrics at our disposal.

As you can see from what they say about their quilt designs (the originals are shown on these pages), each revisited quilt in new colourways presented each quilter with a different and unique set of challenges. This is the fun of having a new set of fabrics to play with each year and why we quilters never tire of our work!

Kaffe Fassett

◀ S Block

Often I feel students make my original version look pale next to the daring combinations of colour they bring to the table. That's definitely the story with *S Block*. I did it in two different colour moods in *Country Garden Quilts*, both rather tonal – one in murky toned stripes and one in many yellow shades of print (left). My workshop students often did it in brilliant contrasts making it a much more lively, graphic design. So I took courage, and using lessons from my students, employed similar bright contrasts to create *Carnival S Block* (see pages 32 and 63), a really scrappy quilt. I love the result. Brandon's strong prints work particularly well in the new version and I think it is more exciting than the original ones.

◀ Star Bouquet

The two versions of this quilt that I did for *Country Garden Quilts* were both bright and contrasting. I decided to make a new version, *Green Star Bouquet* (see pages 30 and 78) that was more tonal. The mood of the new one is of a cool aquarium of watery teals, turquoise and jade greens with flickers of magenta, like tropical fish swimming by, and I like the new version better than my original (left). It's a great quilt to show off your big prints and the crisp star sashing to frame them works a treat. In my first version I used a high pastel palette, but in the new one I have gone for a smoulder of mid-greens with cobalt accents. Imagine taking this symphony of greens and mauves out to picnic in the garden! I could also see bowls of fruit, lime green plates and blue goblets used to ramp up the colour theme. The effect is like a cool mossy bank by a little stream in high summer.

Frames ▶

My temperature really rose when I came up with two new versions, *Blue Frames* (see pages 22 and 69) and *Red Frames* (see pages 24 and 66) of the original *Frames* quilt from *Quilts in the Sun* (right). In the blue one, the frames of dark Indian Stripe and Brandon's Printed Stripes create a sense of mystery, showcasing the deepest colourways of my own prints. Grouping dark fabrics together without any light contrast brings out their glowing qualities. In the red one, the brilliant red really sizzles. I took all the hot reds and oranges from the Shot Cotton collection, adding a few small prints to frame the centre blocks. A sassy magenta pink plays well with red tones. So I've thrown the pink colourway of my Field Bouquet into the mix here. Since I did not have quite enough red and pink tones in my shot cotton range I added Aboriginal Dots and Brandon's Babble fabrics for the frames. The result is a little like red handkerchiefs.

Blue Star ▶

The new version, *Sunshine Stars* (see pages 38 and 89), is simpler and easier to digest than the original in *Caravan of Quilts* (right). I like the way Brandon's prints (like Petra) work in the new design. The limes and peaches go well with all those lemon yellow shades. Wanting a yellow-biased quilt, I picked every yellow fabric in the current Kaffe Collection. Pink, particularly soft candy pink, sits very happily with yellow, as does lime green, so I added shades of these. The polka dots, plaids and stripes add a jaunty rhythm to the ensemble. Repeating the stars gives me the chance to see how different a magenta and green Map star on pink looks rather than on soft mint green. Using different parts of a print like Field Bouquet makes it look like the multiple print that it was designed to be. I enjoyed clarifying the stars by giving them just one textured colour for their backgrounds, making each read better.

Big Bang ▶

I love the *Big Bang* quilt design! As I did it the first time in *Caravan of Quilts* (right), I wanted to have another go at two different versions, deepening the palette and treating it in a more tonal way in one version, *Earthy Big Bang* (see pages 28 and 75) and going quite pale in the other, *Pastel Big Bang* (see pages 26 and 72). I feel the results are quite different from the original. *Earthy Big Bang* is as organic as an autumn tree while *Pastel Big Bang* is as fresh as a line of laundry. I'd love to go on to do a red version or a dark jewel-like one with black and rich deep tones, perhaps using some Marquee Stripe fabric.

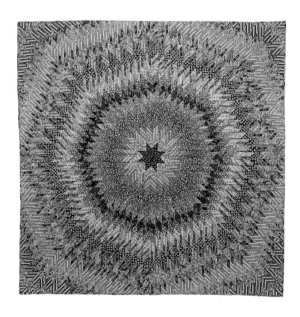

◄ Chevrons

The original quilt in *Quilt Road* was done in a muted palette (left). Here I have recreated the design in two versions, each very different from the original. *Marquee Chevrons* (see pages 34 and 86) is the real surprise. The Marquee Stripe fabric is stunning to use in it. Once I had designed this bold Marquee Stripe for my last fabric collection I was visualizing it used in just such a graphic three-dimensional way. With three colourways of the print you get all these possibilities. Adding Brandon's Wrinkle fabric as the border emphasized the clean simplicity of the stripes.

The rich honey and amber tones of my new Indian Woven Stripes makes the other version, *Rich Chevrons* (see pages 36 and 82) just that in my opinion. The result has a glowing golden palette that should give warmth to any room. I love the way the placement of dark and light in it creates pyramid shapes.

◄ Chintz

The new version, *Garden Chintz* (see pages 40 and 92) has an autumn feel with its earthy browns and golds, the flickers of pale green and lavender giving it a bit of air. In it our new leafy prints work so well. The original design, taken from an Australian chintz quilt, used lots of prints with cream grounds in my first attempt in *Country Garden Quilts* (left). I decided to try an earthier golden-brown palette for the new one. The mirror imaging is very helpful when laying out the design. I like the way the corner pieces almost fade into the leafy and floral prints, just as they did in the Australian original. Philip Jacobs' Miami, a big exotic plant print on lavender, makes just the right impact for the centre panel. You could also create this with a lot more contrast, perhaps using different colourways of the prints that I've chosen.

◄ Cutting Corners

It was very exciting to redo this quilt in a totally different fashion. The original version in *Quilt Romance* used a very limited palette but created excitement by sending the striped angles in a wacky dance of lines (left). After creating my bold Marquee design, I wanted to play with it and use the multi-colours of the stripe in a simple but surprising way. In the new *Crazy Cutting Corners* (see pages 20 and 60) it's thrilling to see how simple squares of coloured stripes on the diagonal can make so many playful forms. It is like a mad tile floor made using a simple diagonal stripe that sometimes contains several colourways of stripe. It proves that however you cut this print, as long as it is on the diagonal, you can create all these variations on squares. The border in the new version uses two colourways only of my Marquee print and looks so different from the woven stripes I used in the original. A really fun quilt to do (for a special tip, see page 61).

Liza Prior Lucy

New Orleans ▶

When I made the this quilt in *Kaleidoscope of Quilts*, I was choosing, cutting and sewing fabric while glued to the television watching the horrible destruction taking place in New Orleans by hurricane Katrina. The colours I was seeing on the screen clearly influenced my choice – muddy greens and greys with dashes of brighter colours scattered about (right). When asked to do a new version, I immediately thought of Mardi Gras, the festival so closely associated with New Orleans, hence the new title *Mardi Gras Star* (see pages 48 and 108). The colours of Mardi Gras are garish green, gold, and purple, so I started there.

Romantic Rosy ▶

This is the first quilt design that Kaffe and I ever did together. The original idea was to use as many floral prints with roses as we could, thus the name. Some years later I did a 'romantic' version for *Quilt Road* that was very popular (right). *Rosy* is the kind of quilt pattern that looks complicated but is actually very fast to make.

For the newest version, *Return to Rosy* (see pages 56 and 124) I just chose my favourite new prints and let them lead the way.

Pastel Gridlock ▶

I love the grey colourway of Philip Jacobs' Glory Rose, so I chose that fabric first to make my new version, *Grey Gridlock* (see pages 58 and 121) of this quilt from *Caravan of Quilts* (right). Silver and grey are currently very popular in home decorating and I studied the colours in magazines to bring about this new colourway.

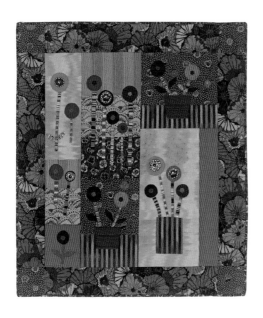

Pauline Smith

◄ *Chelsea*

For my new version, *Summer Chelsea* (see pages 45 and 100) I wanted to capture the essence of the original in *Quilts in the Sun* (left). Whereas some quilters seize the opportunity to make their own fabric choices, others want to make a quilt as near to the original as possible and are daunted when the original fabrics are no longer available. With *Summer Chelsea* I used some of the original fabrics that have now been reintroduced.

For me the most important thing was to get the dark and light rectangles balanced to give the quilt a strong structure. Once I had decided on gold Aboriginal Dot everything else fell into place. Although the Lotus Leaf fabric used for the first version is still available, I chose Kaffe's red Radiation print as I like the way the circular design relates to the flower heads.

◄ *African Huts*

With my new version, *Dusky African Huts* (see pages 55 and 118), my intention was to change the palette of the original quilt in *Quilt Road* as little as possible. I used the Indian Stripes for the huts, just as I did in the first version. The difficulty then was finding a substitute for the yellow Ikat fabric. Time for a re-think! I used the new Woven Indian Stripes with shot cottons and small prints, added more purples, blues and reds, and took out the yellows as they looked too harsh against the other colours. The result is a richly coloured quilt that I really like.

Roberta Horton

◄ *Matisse Villa*

In my new version, *Hot Matisse Villa* (see pages 50 and 111), I tried to recapture the first quilt from *Kaleidoscope of Quilts* (left). Once I compose a quilt, that is the only way I tend to see it. The process of trying to duplicate the feeling of *Matisse Villa* was almost harder than making the original quilt. It is easier to start with a clean slate, not knowing where you are going and then being satisfied when you reach the end of the journey. As I add the choices, working from the centre to the outsides of the quilt, one fabric is selected to balance, or contrast, with another in the composition. I feel contrasts allow you better to see each fabric. For example, florals counter a more angular fabric, like a stripe.

For the border I used Kaffe's Radiation to replace the diagonal stripes used in the original quilt.

Brandon Mably

My Fair Lady ▶

There is nothing more exciting than adding a new life to an old structure. Often we are asked where we get our ideas from. Traditional quilts from the past are a never-ending source and a great way for us to play with my bold graphic patterns giving the play of pattern and design a new twist. For my new version, *Driftwood My Fair Lady* (see pages 46 and 104) of the original quilt from *Quilt Road* (right), I used my latest range of fabrics. I maintained a muted, earthy tone throughout, held down by my grey Shingles fabric for the background but with hints of hot lime and cool powder blue from my Petra fabric design to add a bit of bling here and there. I'm absolutely charmed by the end result and hope you will be too.

Two Up, Two Down ▶

Twilight Two Up, Two Down (see pages 52 and 114) follows on from my original quilt shot in the charming Port Meirion village in North Wales, with its rich pastel painted walls (featured in *Quilt Romance*). My happy colours in the original colourway (right) worked very well there but knowing that for this book we would be photographing in the more subdued setting of a farming village in Bulgaria, surrounded by warm, earthy tones, I couldn't resist playing with a richer, moody, darker look for my new design. Using my dark Dapple fabric with the rich magenta dots for the back ground, I threw in a kick of colours in hot reds, greens and midnight blues for the houses, giving the whole quilt a very different look indeed. My first colourway resembles a sunny day-time palette and the new one is more like dusk; it has a playful intrigue about it.

Mary Mashuta

All Season Garden ▶

I often enjoy re-using a quilt block that fascinates me with completely new fabric choices. I have gained an understanding of how the block works so it's fun to see just how different it can look the second or third time. In the first go-around with the *All Season Garden* quilt in *Quilt Road* (right), the fabrics combined magically, or at least that's what it seemed like in retrospect. However in my new version, *Dotty All Season Garden* (see pages 42 and 96) it was a huge challenge as there were numerous colourways of five different fabrics to consider – a real 'headful' – but the effect is very pleasing.

the new fabrics

Kaffe discusses the new designs (by himself, Philip Jacobs and Brandon Mably) in the Kaffe Fassett Collection. Kaffe's fabrics are shown on pages 14–15, Philip's on pages 16–17 and Brandon's on pages 18–19.

Kaffe Fassett

Shirt Stripes (below)
This design was inspired by seeing stripes of different scales on the pages of a scrapbook at a vintage fabric sale. I am reworking it by popular demand.

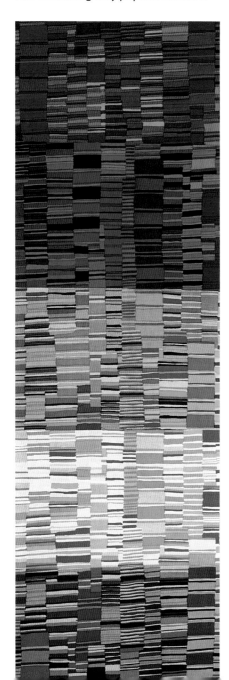

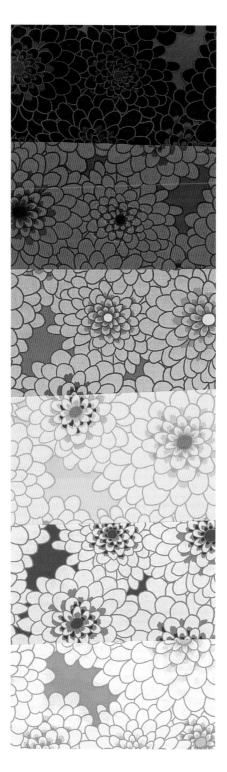

Field Bouquet (above)
The bold, naïve flowers in a heavily embroidered vintage quilt fascinated me, and I thought I'd create this effect for quilters who didn't have the time or the skill to embroider flowers. (See page 67 for special cutting techniques).

Line Dance (left)
Studying Japanese kimono designs, I noticed they often stylize the flower forms to create even petals radiating from a central circle. I grabbed that idea and overlapped many versions of it in different scales.

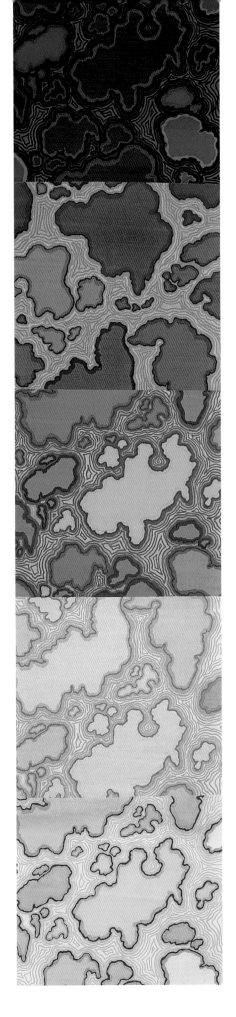

This was the last design I did for this collection. I needed a showstopper after the more textural ideas I had produced thus far. The overlapping 1920s' style flowers I'd seen in old English needlepoints were my inspiration. I love the flat variations that ended up looking almost Art Deco in mood.

Folk Art (above)
When I was in Sweden recently I kept seeing shopping bags with green shapes on them. The effect was fresh and intriguing so I thought it would make a good patchwork fabric. The two-colour simplicity should create a good injection of tone for a quilt.

Map (left)
I've always loved old maps and it was only a matter of time before I used these organic island shapes in a print.

Philip Jacobs

Begonia Columns (below)
This very large-scale leaf stripe is exciting when cut in pieces for patchwork, but would also make wonderful leafy sashings for a quilt. We use it as a dramatic backing to great effect.

Lacy (right)
This reminded me of vintage endpapers or Japanese kimono fabric. I can never get enough circles and this is a great addition to those already in the Kaffe collection. Combine them all for exciting, repetitive forms in a quilt.

Moon Flower (above)
Morning glories are one of my favourite flowers. These larger-than-life ones make such an exciting drama, adding to our collection of circles prints. This fabric design fussy cuts a treat for bold effect.

16

Miami (below)
A lovely bit of tropical camp for our collection. I coloured it with those banana-tree wallpapers and fabrics you see in Florida in mind, hence the name.

Floating Mums (below)
These voluptuous blooms on a brocade ground can be fussy cut very effectively or just used in large or small geometric shapes, such as diamonds. The scale is perfect for creating the drama I love to see on floral fabrics.

Scallops (above)
The never ending variety of pattern and colour you see on shells makes it one of nature's most intriguing images. I love the overall shape, overlapping most satisfyingly in this print. It is rich as a border or a square, and is wonderful as a backing.

Brandon Mably

Shingles (below)
Images of fish scales, ripples on water and tiled roofs combined together to lead to this overlapping small-scale pattern. It works well as a background for other prints.

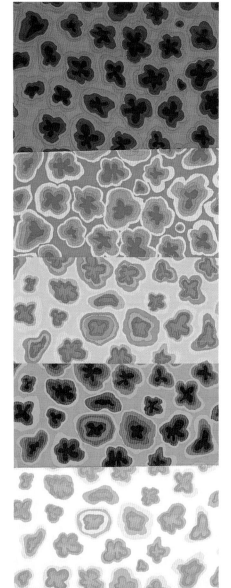

Plaid (below)
This is Brandon's homage to tartan, Burberry checks and any grid-like pattern. With its primitive brush strokes, this design cuts up beautifully and works well with his other prints.

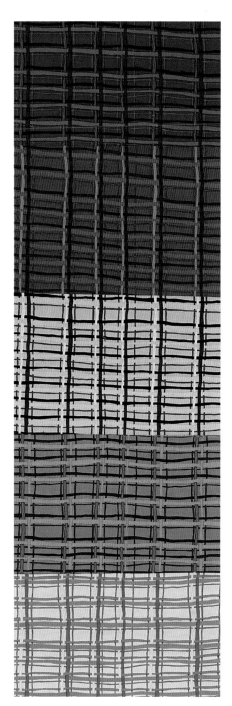

Petra (above)
As Brandon was walking through the British Museum, a marble slab with this overall pattern resembling keyholes with radiating outlines caught his eye. He couldn't resist painting out his interpretation for a fabric.

Rope (below)
A girlfriend of Brandon's from Scotland showed him a picture she took of a pile of pink rope on her brother's fishing boat. Brandon thought this would make an interesting print, so he took the swirling curves of the rope and added dots for shading. He's thrilled with the result.

Macaroni (above)
Brandon is a keen cook and loves pasta dishes. The primitive, wacky round form of wagon-wheel shapes called out to him as an all-over print that would cut up nicely.

Useful information

CUTTING TECHNIQUES

Field Bouquet has four different square panels (each measuring 10in/25.5cm) that run across the width of the fabric. They are are surrounded by sufficient background to allow for fussy cutting. To this end, the quantities of fabrics required in the *Red Frames* and *Sunshine Stars* quilts are given in numbers of strips of panels, not in yards or metres.

SOME EXAMPLES OF QUILTS IN WHICH THE NEW FABRICS ARE USED

Kaffe's fabrics
Shirt Stripes (See *Grey Gridlock* on pages 58 and 121)
Map (See *Earthy Big Bang* on pages 28 and 75)
Line Dance (See *Red Frames* on pages 24 and 66)
Folk Art (See *Carnival S Block* on pages 32 and 63)
Kite Tails (See *Pastel Big Bang* on pages 26 and 72)

Philip's fabrics
Begonia Columns (See *Blue Frames* on pages 22 and 69)
Lacy (See *Return To Rosy* on pages 56 and 124)
Moon Flower (See *Garden Chintz* on pages 40 and 92)
Miami (See *Grey Gridlock* on pages 58 and 121)
Scallops (See *Sunshine Stars* on pages 38 and 89)
Floating Mums (See *Mardi Gras Star* on pages 48 and 108)

Brandon's fabrics
Macaroni (See *Driftwood My Fair Lady* on pages 46 and 104)
Petra (See *Sunshine Stars* on pages 38 and 89)
Shingles (See *Driftwood My Fair Lady* on pages 46 and 104)
Rope (See *Driftwood My Fair Lady* on pages 46 and 104 and *Sunshine Stars* on pages 38 and 89)

Crazy Cutting Corners
by Kaffe Fassett

The new version of my *Cutting Corners* quilt, using my
Marquee stripe, looks really dramatic with these Bulgarian
watermelons and against the luscious peaches. It seems
stripes just get more and more exciting in fashion, furnishing
and quilting.

Blue Frames
by Kaffe Fassett

The blue version of my *Frames* quilt positively glows against the rich turquoise painted door and the blue bike blends right in. The leaves and blooms in our prints are just the right scale. I'm impressed with how well our handwoven stripes from India work with our prints in this saturated blue palette.

Red Frames
by Kaffe Fassett

It always sends a shiver up my spine when clear, deep magenta joins forces with scarlet. In fact, multiple shades of red and pink tones will vibrate wonderfully and look good in the *Red Frames* version of this quilt on an old tram carriage in the village. The Serape stripe backing works a treat as well.

Pastel Big Bang
by Kaffe Fassett

This monumental church
entrance was too good a
setting to resist for this
version of *Big Bang*. The
celestial blues really sing
in harmony here. I love the
way the opal-like paleness
of this quilt contrasts with
the earth brown colourway
on page 28.

red wood and

eally glow

rint in rust

bric adds a rich

racotta palette

Green Star Bouquet
by Kaffe Fassett

These silvery blue-green cabbages, the terracotta tiled roof and dark weathered barn make such a perfect setting for this version of the *Star Bouquet* quilt in cobalt and cool greens with shots of magenta. Philip Jacobs' oversized Begonia Column print makes a dramatic backing. I also like the perky Guinea Flower binding.

Carnival S Block
by Kaffe Fassett

Inspired by students in my workshops, I made this new *S Block* quilt a lot more contrasty and bright. It's sassiness looks right at home in this old farm courtyard. Philip Jacobs' Japanese Chrysanthemum fabric is wonderfully rich on the backing.

Marquee Chevrons
by Kaffe Fassett

The Art Deco green and white door creates a strong echo of the new *Chevrons* quilt made in the Marquee Stripe. You can just glimpse the grape arbour – nearly every house in the village makes their own brandy from their grapes.

Rich Chevrons
by Kaffe Fassett

In this second version of the *Chevron* quilt I used mostly my handwoven Indian stripes in a warm amber palette. My Map fabric makes a rich backing, as you can see, held her by one of the village woman. What about that jacket of hers!

Sunshine Stars
by Kaffe Fassett

The yellow gold of this freshly harvested corn melts with my *Star* quilt. The hot yellows, reds, lavenders and limes and the cool sky blue of the quilt respond excitingly with this mass of rich gold. The colours of the local village taxi, which we loved, blend with it.

Garden Chintz
by Kaffe Fassett

This new version of my *Chintz* quilt almost dissolves in the glowing light and earthy tones of this Bulgarian barn. Those onions are a visual feast. Philip Jacobs' Begonia Columns adds great style used as backing. And these singing Morning Glories echo Philip Jacobs' Morning Glory print most lusciously.

Dotty All Season Garden
by Mary Mashuta

This lushly glowing farmhouse makes Mary Mashuta's new version of this quilt look right at home. Her lively, but mellow colour palette is just perfect below these grape leaves.

Summer Chelsea
by Pauline Smith

Pauline Smith's jaunty flower shapes in her new *Chelsea* quilt respond to the rustic pole fence and gate and to the patch of bright zinnias. I love the way Pauline plays with circular motifs in the prints and her appliqué Lollipop flowers.

Driftwood My Fair Lady
by Brandon Mably

The original *My Fair Lady* was done in sweet pastels on a grey background. Brandon has picked a husky, neutral palette, mostly in his own prints, for this new version. The soft greys, beiges and muted apricot tones are so at home with this rustic farmyard. The backing is in Brandon's powerful Rope design.

Mardi Gras Star
by Liza Prior Lucy

The jazzy palette of Liza Lucy's new *Star* quilt sits perfectly on this mellow gold farm wagon with its leaf-green wheels. It is usually attached to a donkey and caught our attention as we walked about the village. Brandon Mably's Babble print makes a good green binding to go with the wheels.

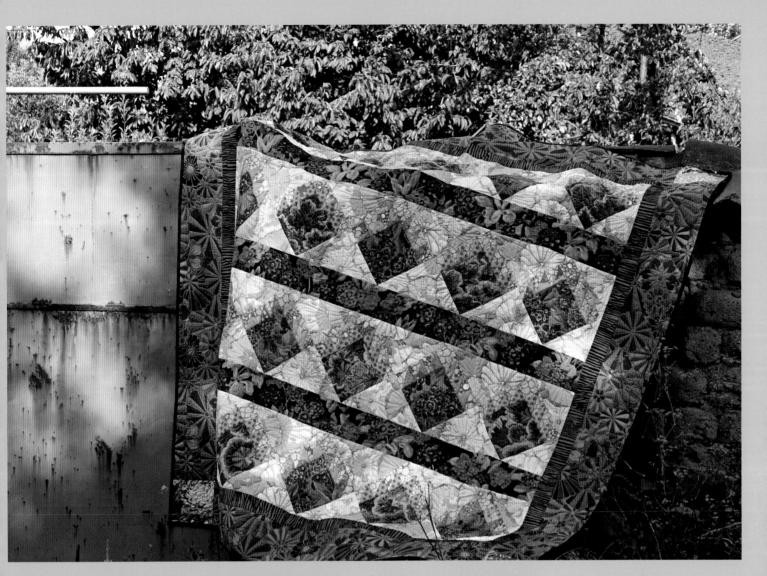

Hot Matisse Villa
by Roberta Horton

This rusty pea-green
farm gate called to us as
we sought a setting for
Roberta's quilt. Her rich use
of contrast works so well
with the weathered paint
and rusty metal.

Twilight Two Up Two Down

by Brandon Mably

Brandon Mably's new quilt looks like it was designed for this farmhouse gate. His deep blue and purple palette with hot red doors and windows is perfectly balanced with the turquoise and orange peeling gate. He loved the spiky old equipment against the wall – a feature of this working village.

Dusky African Huts
by Pauline Smith

Pauline Smith's new *African Huts* found such a good home
in this farmhouse vegetable patch with hot zinnias and
geraniums. We love the jars of preserved peppers and
tomatoes. The Indian Stripes really shine in this quilt.

Return To Rosy
by Liza Prior Lucy

This elegant antique-toned farmyard was one of my favourite settings in the village. The stone, weathered wood and chickens make Liza's new version of this rustic quilt glow quite softly. Kite Tails is the perfect backing fabric.

Grey Gridlock
by Liza Prior Lucy

The original *Gridlock* was inspired by a piece of knitting. Here we see Liza's new pastel version of the deeper original. The soft florals in mint green, aqua and lavender create a cool freshness. The weathered, frosty green gate is the perfect foil for this quilt.

crazy cutting corners *

Kaffe Fassett

The centre of this stunning quilt is made using just 2 fabrics. Kaffe's Marquee fabrics incorporate 6 different colour combinations of striped blocks repeated across the fabric width. The fabrics are cut into squares (Template NN) on the bias (diagonal) and therefore require careful handling to prevent stretching. The quilt centre is framed with a pieced border using a triangle (Template OO) with plain corner posts (Template NN).

SIZE OF QUILT
The finished quilt will measure approx. 80in x 80in (203cm x 203cm).

MATERIALS
Patchwork Fabrics
MARQUEE
Bright   GP121BT   2 3/8yd (2.2m)
Husky   GP121HU   4 1/2yd (4.1m)
SHOT COTTON
Chartreuse   SC12   1 1/8yd (1m)

Backing Fabric 6yd (5.5m)
We suggest these fabrics for backing
SHIRT STRIPES Red, GP51RD
MARQUEE Bright, GP121BT

Binding
MARQUEE
Husky   GP121HU   3/4yd (70cm)

Batting
88in x 88in (223.5cm x 223.5cm).

Quilting thread
Toning hand quilting thread.

Templates

NN   OO

CUTTING DIAGRAM FOR GP121HU

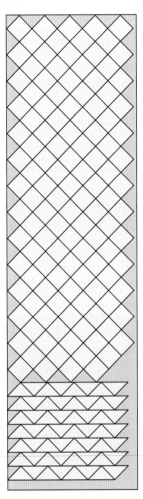

CUTTING OUT
As the Marquee fabrics have so much colour variation we have simplified the diagram for this quilt to show only the position of the fabrics. Please refer to the photograph for help with stripe directions and colour combinations. We recommend making clear plastic templates and drawing out the shapes onto the fabric before cutting. We have also provided a cutting diagram for fabric GP121HU to show how the shapes are arranged.
Template NN Marquee Fabrics only With the stripes running on the diagonal (corner to corner) cut 121 squares 5 1/2in x 5 1/2in (14cm x 14cm) in GP121HU and 75 in GP121BT. Total 196 squares.
Template NN Cut 4 squares 5 1/2in x 5 1/2in (14cm x 14cm) in SC12 for border corner posts.
Template OO Marquee Fabric only Cut 4 1/8in (10.5cm) strips across the width of the fabric, each strip will give you 8 triangles per full width. With the stripes running on the diagonal cut 56 triangles in GP121HU.
Template OO Cut 5 7/8in (15cm) strips across the width of the fabric, each strip will give you 12 triangles per full width. Cut 56 in SC12.

Binding Cut 9 strips 2 1/2in (6.5cm) wide across the width of the fabric in GP121HU.

Backing Cut 2 pieces 40in x 88in (101.5cm x 223.5cm), 2 pieces 40in x 9in (101.5cm x 22.75cm) and 1 piece 9in x 9in (22.75cm x 22.75cm) in backing fabric.

MAKING THE QUILT
Handle your cut squares carefully as they have bias cut edges and will be stretchy. Lay out the squares with the stripe directions running alternately using a design wall, move them around until you have a pleasing combination, then piece them into 14 rows of 14 squares. Use plenty of pins to assist in piecing the bias edges. Join the rows to form the quilt centre.

Kaffe says:
What I suggest for this wild quilt is to cut the stripe squares however they present themselves on the fabric; some will be purely two colour stripes, but most will be an interesting mix. Slap them up on your design wall (or place on the floor) then look at them through your camera or a reducing glass and see where the lighter squares are building up. Too many together, creating too light an area? Disperse these so they are a little more evenly spread across the quilt. Then create some formations of squares on point by placing three or four squares with the same diagonal colour – only a few are needed to give the mood of the geometry of the design, so let the others be 'maverick'. I have just realized you could do a version of this in my Woven Stripes fabric from India.

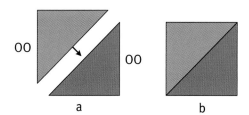

OO   OO

a   b

MAKING THE BORDER

Piece the template OO triangles into squares as shown in border block assembly diagram a. The finished border block is shown in diagram b. Make 56 blocks and join them into 4 borders of 14 blocks. Add a border to each side of the quilt. Add a corner post to each end of the 2 remaining borders then join these to the quilt top and bottom as shown in the quilt assembly diagram.

FINISHING THE QUILT

Press the quilt top. Seam the backing pieces using a ¼in (6mm) seam allowance to form a piece approx. 88in x 88in (223.5cm x 223.5cm). Layer the quilt top, batting and backing and baste together (see page 140). Using toning hand quilting thread, quilt 4 or 5 diagonal lines across each square following the fabric stripes. Trim the quilt edges and attach the binding (see page 141).

QUILT ASSEMBLY DIAGRAM

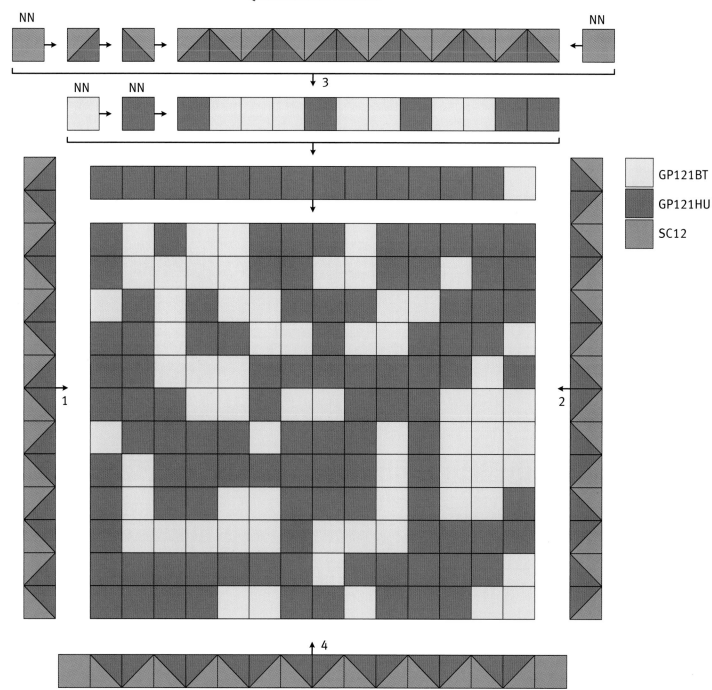

GP121BT

GP121HU

SC12

carnival s block **

Kaffe Fassett

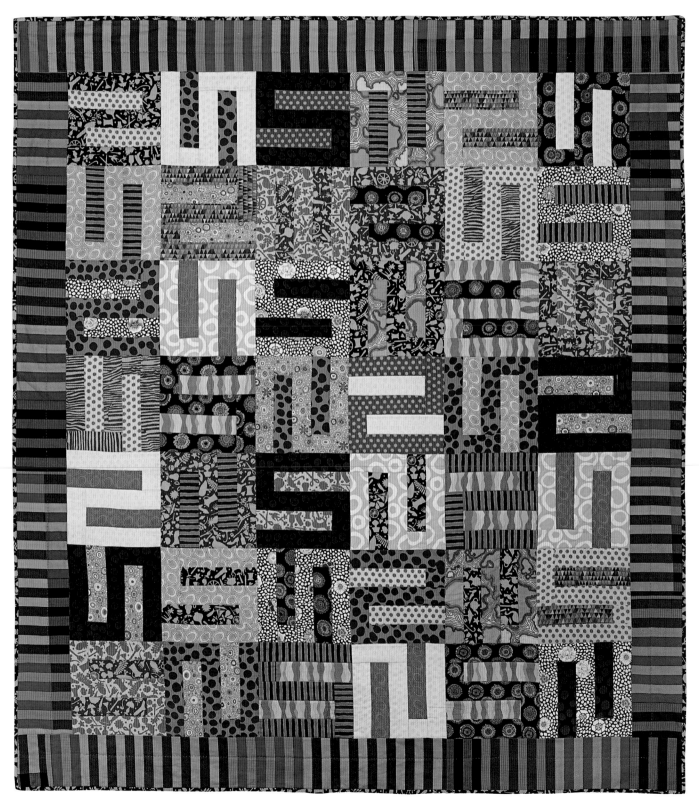

The interesting 'S' blocks which form the centre of this quilt are pieced using 3 rectangles (Templates AA, BB and CC) and a square (Template DD). The blocks finish to 10in (25.5cm) and are pieced in 2 ways (see Block Diagrams). Block 2 is a mirror image of block 1. They are straight set into rows and then surrounded by a simple border to complete the quilt.

SIZE OF QUILT
The finished quilt will measure approx. 71in x 81in (180.5cm x 206cm).

MATERIALS
Patchwork Fabrics
TENTS
Driftwood	BM03DR	¼yd (25cm)

WAVES
Desert	BM04DS	¼yd (25cm)

DAPPLE
Animal	BM05AM	½yd (45cm)
Regal	BM05RE	½yd (45cm)

FISH LIPS
Lilac	BM07LI	¼yd (25cm)

STRAWS
Midnight	BM08MD	⅜yd (35cm)

WRINKLE
Brown	BM18BR	¼yd (25cm)

ROMAN GLASS
Gold	GP01GD	¼yd (25cm)

GUINEA FLOWER
Green	GP59GN	½yd (45cm)

SPOT
Apple	GP70AL	⅜yd (35cm)
Gold	GP70GD	⅜yd (35cm)
Red	GP70RD	¼yd (25cm)

ABORIGINAL DOTS
Lilac	GP71LI	⅜yd (35cm)
Orange	GP71OR	¼yd (25cm)

PLINK
Black	GP109BK	½yd (45cm)

FOLK ART
Black	GP119BK	⅜yd (35cm)
Pink	GP119PK	¼yd (25cm)
Rust	GP119RU	⅜yd (35cm)

MAP
Brown	GP120BR	¼yd (25cm)

Border Fabric
MARQUEE
Husky	GP121HU	1½yd (1.4m)

Backing Fabric 5⅜yd (4.9m)
We suggest these fabrics for backing
JAPANESE CRYSANTHEMUM Red, PJ 41RD
TENTS Driftwood, BM04DR
SPOT Apple, GP70AL

Binding
FOLK ART
Black	GP119BK	⅝yd (60cm)

Batting
79in x 89in (200.5cm x 226cm).

Quilting thread
Toning machine quilting thread and pink perlé embroidery thread

Templates

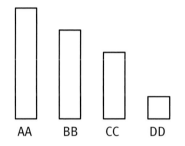

AA   BB   CC   DD

CUTTING OUT
Cut the fabric in the order stated to prevent waste, use leftover strips for later templates as appropriate.

Template AA Cut 2½in (6.25cm) strips across the width of the fabric. Each strip will give you 3 rectangles per width. Cut 4 in BM05AM, BM05RE, GP59GN, 3 in BM07LI, GP70AL, GP71LI, GP109BK, GP119RU, 2 in BM08MD, GP70GD, GP119BK, GP119PK, GP120BR, 1 in BM03DR, BM04DS, BM18BR, GP01GD and GP70RD. Total 42 Rectangles.

Template BB Cut 2½in (6.25cm) strips across the width of the fabric. Each strip will give you 4 rectangles per width. Cut 12 BM05AM, BM05RE, BM08MD, GP109BK, 10 in BM04DS, GP01GD, GP59GN, GP70AL, GP70GD, GP119BK, GP119RU, 8 in GP71LI, GP71OR, GP119PK, 6 in BM03DR, BM07LI, GP120BR, 4 in BM18BR and GP70RD. Total 168 Rectangles.

Template CC Cut 2½in (6.25cm) strips across the width of the fabric or use leftover strips from previous templates. Cut 4 in BM05AM, BM05RE, GP59GN, 3 in BM07LI, GP70AL, GP71LI, GP109BK, GP119RU, 2 in BM08MD, GP70GD, GP119BK, GP119PK, GP120BR, 1 in BM03DR, BM04DS, BM18BR, GP01GD and GP70RD. Total 42 Rectangles.

Template DD Cut 2½in (6.25cm) strips across the width of the fabric or use leftover strips from previous templates. Cut 4 in BM05AM, BM05RE, GP59GN, 3 in BM07LI, GP70AL, GP71LI, GP109BK, GP119RU, 2 in BM08MD, GP70GD, GP119BK, GP119PK, GP120BR, 1 in BM03DR, BM04DS, BM18BR, GP01GD and GP70RD. Total 42 Rectangles.

Border Cut 8 strips 6in (15.25cm) across the width of fabric in GP121HU. Join as necessary and cut 2 strips 6in x 71½in (15.25cm x 181.5cm) for the top and bottom of the quilt and 2 strips 6in x 70½in (15.25cm x 179cm) for the sides of the quilt.

Binding Cut 8 strips 2½in (6.5cm) wide across the width of the fabric in GP119BK.

Backing Cut 2 pieces 40in x 89in (101.5cm x 226cm) in backing fabric.

MAKING THE BLOCKS
Use a ¼in (6mm) seam allowance throughout. Refer to the quilt assembly diagram and photograph for fabric

BLOCK DIAGRAMS

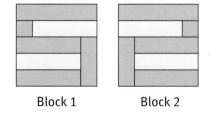

Block 1   Block 2

BLOCK ASSEMBLY DIAGRAMS

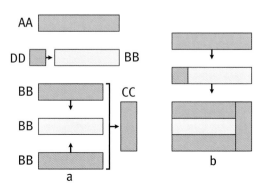

a   b

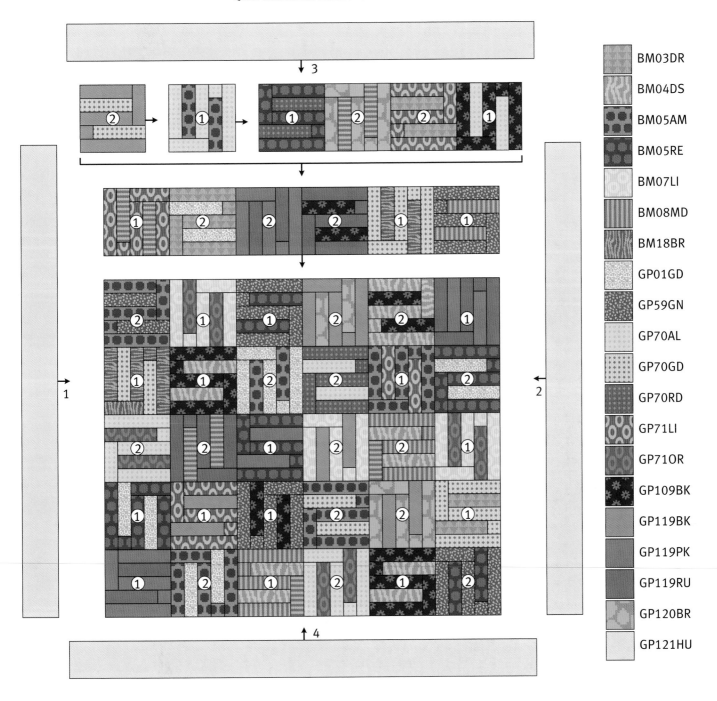

	BM03DR
	BM04DS
	BM05AM
	BM05RE
	BM07LI
	BM08MD
	BM18BR
	GP01GD
	GP59GN
	GP70AL
	GP70GD
	GP70RD
	GP71LI
	GP71OR
	GP109BK
	GP119BK
	GP119PK
	GP119RU
	GP120BR
	GP121HU

placement and block type. Each block is made of a main fabric and a background fabric. There are 2 block types, block 1 and block 2, as shown in the block diagrams. Follow block assembly diagrams a and b to piece 21 of Block 1. Use the same technique to piece 21 of block 2 which are a mirror image of block 1.

MAKING THE QUILT
Lay out the blocks as shown in the quilt assembly diagram. The blocks are rotated in alternating positions. Join the blocks into 7 rows of 6 blocks, then join the rows to form the quilt centre. Add the side borders, then top and bottom borders to the quilt centre as indicated in the quilt assembly diagram to complete the quilt.

FINISHING THE QUILT
Press the quilt top. Seam the backing pieces using a ¼in (6mm) seam allowance to form a piece approx 79in x 89in (200.5cm x 226cm). Layer the quilt top, batting and backing and baste together (see page 140). Using toning machine quilting thread, quilt the ditch in all the seams. In the border hand quilt a line 2in (5cm) outside the seam line using pink perlé embroidery thread. Trim the quilt edges and attach the binding (see page 141).

red frames *

Kaffe Fassett

The block centres in this quilt are simple squares (Square) surrounded with a wide frame made using 2 rectangles (Long and Short Rectangle), all are cut to size and no templates are provided for this very simple design. The blocks, which finish to 15in (38cm) are set in straight rows to complete the quilt top. Kaffe chose his Field Bouquet fabrics for this quilt, the panels in the fabric design are perfect in the plainer frames. Extra fabric has been allowed for fussy cutting the panels.

SIZE OF QUILT
The finished quilt will measure approx. 75in x 75in (190.5cm x 190.5cm).

MATERIALS
Patchwork Fabrics

BABBLE		
Red	BM13RD	¾yd (70cm)
HERRINGBONE STRIPE		
Red	BM19RD	½yd (45cm)
ABORIGINAL DOTS		
Purple	GP71PU	½yd (45cm)
Red	GP71RD	⅝yd (60cm)
Terracotta	GP71TC	½yd (45cm)
ASIAN CIRCLES		
Tomato	GP89TM	⅜yd (35cm)
COGS		
Red	GP110RD	⅜yd (35cm)
RADIATION		
Red	GP115RD	⅜yd (35cm)
LINE DANCE		
Red	GP116RD	⅜yd (35cm)
FIELD BOUQUET		
Pink	GP118PK	2 strips of panels
Red	GP118RD	2 strips of panels
KITE TAILS		
Red	GP122RD	⅜yd (35cm)
FLOATING MUMS		
Red	PJ49RD	⅜yd (35cm)
SHOT COTTON		
Ginger	SC01	⅝yd (60cm)
Persimmon	SC07	⅜yd (35cm)
Raspberry	SC08	⅜yd (35cm)
Scarlet	SC44	½yd (45cm)
Clementine	SC80	½yd (45cm)
Magenta	SC81	⅝yd (60cm)

Backing Fabric 5¼yd (4.8m)
We suggest these fabrics for backing
SERAPE Red, GP111RD
Or any of the shot cottons used in the quilt

Binding
WOVEN BROAD STRIPE
Red   WBS RD   ⅝yd (60cm)

Batting
83in x 83in (211cm x 211cm)

Quilting thread
Deep pink perlé embroidery thread

Templates

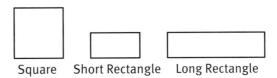

Square   Short Rectangle   Long Rectangle

CUTTING OUT
Cut the fabric in the order stated.
Squares Cut 8in (20.25cm) squares. Fussy cut 8 panels in GP118RD and 5 in GP118PK. Cut 3 in PG49RD, 2 in GP89TM, GP110RD, GP115RD, GP122RD and 1 in GP116RD. Total 25 squares.
Long Rectangles Cut 4¼in (10.75cm) strips across the width of the fabric. Cut 4¼in x 15½in (10.75cm x 39.5cm) rectangles. Cut 8 in BM13RD, 6 in GP71RD, SC01, SC81, 4 in GP71PU, GP71RD, SC44, SC80, 2 in SC07 and SC08, also fussy cut 4 in BM19RD with the stripes running down the length of the rectangle. Total 50 rectangles. Reserve the left over strips for the Short Rectangles.
Short Rectangles Cut 4¼in (10.75cm) strips across the width of the fabric. Cut 4¼in x 8in (10.75cm x 20.25cm) rectangles. Also use the leftovers from the Long Rectangles. Cut 8 in BM13RD, 6 in GP71RD, SC01, SC81, 4 in GP71PU, GP71RD, SC44, SC80, 2 in SC07 and SC08, also fussy cut 4 in BM19RD with the stripes running down the length of the rectangle. Total 50 rectangles.

Binding Cut 8 strips 2½in (6.5cm) across the width of the fabric in WBS RD.

Backing Cut 2 pieces 40in x 83in (101.5cm x 211cm), 2 pieces 40in x 4in (101.5cm x 10.25cm) and 1 piece 4in x 4in (10.25cm x 10.25cm) in backing fabric. For a quirky look to the backing you could cut the 4in (10.25cm) square from a different fabric and piece the backing with the contrasting square in the centre.

MAKING THE BLOCKS
Use a ¼in (6mm) seam allowance throughout. Referring to the quilt assembly diagram for fabric placement piece 25 blocks as shown in block assembly diagram a, the finished block can be seen in diagram b. Note that the position of the long and short rectangles alternates across the whole quilt.

BLOCK ASSEMBLY DIAGRAMS

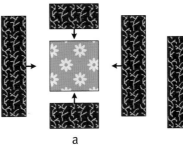

a   b

MAKING THE QUILT

Join the blocks into 5 rows of 5 blocks as shown in the quilt assembly diagram. Join the rows to complete the quilt.

FINISHING THE QUILT

Press the quilt top. Seam the backing pieces using a ¼in (6mm) seam allowance to form a piece approx. 83in x 83in (211cm x 211cm). Layer the quilt top, batting and backing and baste together (see page 140). Using deep pink perlé embroidery thread, quilt 2 parallel lines in the frames, spaced at 1¼in and 2½in (3.25cm and 6.25cm) from the block centres, and a 4¼in (10.75cm) diameter circle in each centre square. Trim the quilt edges and attach the binding (see page 141).

QUILT ASSEMBLY DIAGRAM

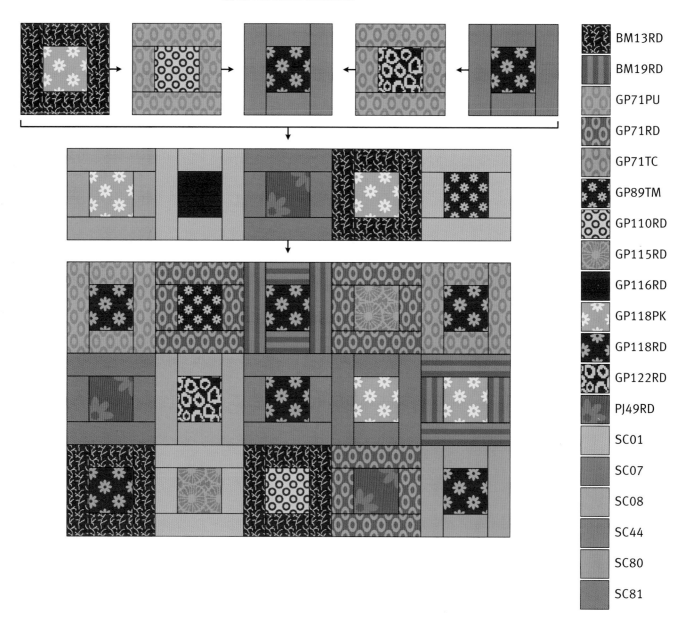

BM13RD
BM19RD
GP71PU
GP71RD
GP71TC
GP89TM
GP110RD
GP115RD
GP116RD
GP118PK
GP118RD
GP122RD
PJ49RD
SC01
SC07
SC08
SC44
SC80
SC81

blue frames *

Kaffe Fassett

The block centres in this quilt are simple squares (Square) surrounded with a wide frame made using 2 rectangles (Long and Short Rectangle), all are cut to size and no templates are provided for this very simple design. The blocks, which finish to 15in (38cm), are set in straight rows to complete the quilt top. Kaffe chose to fussy cut stripe fabrics for the frames in this version, with the stripes running around the centre square. The stripe fabrics are cut down the length of the fabric so please read the cutting instructions carefully.

SIZE OF QUILT
The finished quilt will measure approx. 75in x 75in (190.5cm x 190.5cm).

MATERIALS
Patchwork Fabrics

STRAWS		
Midnight	BM08MD	1¼yd (1.15m)
WRINKLE		
Black	BM18BK	¾yd (70cm)
ZINNIA		
Blue	GP31BL	⅜yd (35cm)
BEKAH		
Cobalt	GP69CB	⅜yd (35cm)
ASIAN CIRCLES		
Dark	GP89DK	⅜yd (35cm)
MAP		
Dark	GP120DK	⅜yd (35cm)
BEGONIA COLUMNS		
Blue	PJ44BL	⅜yd (35cm)
LACY		
Dark	PJ46DK	⅜yd (35cm)
MIAMI		
Cobalt	PJ47CB	⅜yd (35cm)
MOON FLOWER		
Blue	PJ48BL	⅜yd (35cm)
FLOATING MUMS		
Purple	PJ49PU	⅜yd (35cm)
WOVEN ALTERNATING STRIPE		
Blue	WAS BL	¾yd (70cm)
WOVEN BROAD STRIPE		
Blue	WBS BL	1¼yd (1.15m)
WOVEN CATERPILLAR STRIPE		
Blue	WCS BL	¾yd (70cm)
WOVEN NARROW STRIPE		
Blue	WNS BL	¾yd (70cm)

Backing Fabric 5¼yd (4.8m)
We suggest these fabrics for backing
SHIRT STRIPES Cobalt, GP51CB
BEKAH Cobalt, GP69CB
MOON FLOWER Blue, PJ48BL

Binding
MILLEFIORE
Blue GP92BL ⅝yd (60cm)

Batting
83in x 83in (211cm x 211cm)

QUILT ASSEMBLY DIAGRAM

	BM08MD
	BM18BK
	GP31BL
	GP69CB
	GP89DK
	GP120DK
	PJ44BL
	PJ46DK
	PJ47CB
	PJ48BL
	PJ49PU
	WAS BL
	WBS BL
	WCS BL
	WNS BL

Quilting thread
Toning machine quilting and purple perlé embroidery threads

Templates
See Red Frames Quilt.

CUTTING OUT
Cut the fabric in the order stated.
Squares Cut 8in (20.25cm) squares.
Cut 4 in PJ47CB, 3 in GP69CB, PJ44BL, PJ46DK, PJ48BL, PJ49PU, 2 in GP31BL, GP89DK, and GP120DK. Total 25 squares.
Long Rectangles Cut 15½in (39.5cm) strips across the width of the fabric.
Cut 4¼in x 15½in (10.75cm x 39.5cm) rectangles. Cut 10 in BM08MD, WBS BL, 8 in BM18BK, WCS BL, WNS BL and 6 in WAS BL. Total 50 rectangles. Reserve the

left over strips for the Short Rectangles.
Short Rectangles Cut 8in (10.75cm) strips across the width of the fabric.
Cut 4¼in x 8in (10.75cm x 20.25cm) rectangles. Also use the leftovers from the Long Rectangles. Cut 10 in BM08MD, WBS BL, 8 in BM18BK, WCS BL, WNS BL and 6 in WAS BL. Total 50 rectangles.

Binding Cut 8 strips 2½in (6.5cm) wide x width of fabric in GP92BL.

Backing Cut 2 pieces 40in x 83in (101.5cm x 211cm), 2 pieces 40in x 4in (101.5cm x 10.25cm) and 1 piece 4in x 4in (10.25cm x 10.25cm) in backing fabric. For a quirky look to the backing you could cut the 4in (10.25cm) square from a different fabric and piece the

backing with the contrasting square in the centre.

MAKING THE BLOCKS
See Red Frames Quilt.

MAKING THE QUILT
See Red Frames Quilt.

FINISHING THE QUILT
See Red Frames Quilt. For this version quilt 4¼in (10.75cm) diameter circles, using purple perlé embroidery thread, in the centre of each square. Then machine quilt in the ditch vertically and horizontally extending the quilting lines straight across the long rectangles to make a grid. Then quilt along the rectangles with a further 2 parallel lines.

pastel big bang ***

Kaffe Fassett

A single diamond patch shape (Template KK) is used for this quilt. The diamonds are pieced into 8 segments, which are joined to make the quilt. The fabrics are used in sequence to create dramatic rings of colour. The quilt is trimmed to a square shape rather than using many small templates for filling the edges.

SIZE OF QUILT
The finished quilt will measure approx.
95in x 95in (241.5cm x 241.5cm).

MATERIALS
Patchwork Fabrics
FISH LIPS
| Lilac | BM07LI | ⅛yd (15cm) |

STRAWS
| Pastel | BM08PT | ½yd (45cm) |

BABBLE
| White | BM13WH | ¾yd (70cm) |

RINGS
| Pastel | BM15PT | 1⅜yd (1.3m) |

WRINKLE
| Blue | BM18BL | ⅝yd (60cm) |

BEADED TENTS
| Pastel | BM20PT | ¾yd (70cm) |

GUINEA FLOWER
| Mauve | GP59MV | ⅜yd (35cm) |

SPOT
Chalk	GP70CH	1yd (90cm)
China Blue	GP70CI	1⅛yd (1m)
Hydrangea	GP70HY	¾yd (70cm)
Sky	GP70SK	¼yd (25cm)

RADIATION
| Pastel | GP115PT | 1¼yd (1.15m) |

LINE DANCE
| Blue | GP116BL | 1¼yd (1.15m) |
| White | GP116WH | ¾yd (70cm) |

OMBRE
| Pastel | GP117PT | 1⅛yd (1m) |

FOLK ART
| Blue | GP119BL | ⅞yd (80cm) |
| White | GP119WH | ¾yd (70cm) |

MAP
| Pastel | GP120PT | ½yd (45cm) |

MARQUEE
| Pastel | GP121PT | ¾yd (70cm) |

Backing Fabric 9⅛yd (8.4m)
We suggest these fabrics for backing
MAP Pastel, GP120PT
LINE DANCE White, GP116WH
GUINEA FLOWER Mauve, GP59MV

Binding Fabric
BABBLE
| Blue | BM13BL | ¾yd (70cm) |

Batting
103in x 103in (261.5cm x 261.5cm)

Quilting threads
Toning machine quilting thread

Templates

KK

CUTTING OUT
Template KK Cut 2¾in (7cm) strips across the width of the fabric. Each strip will give you 9 diamonds per full width. Cut 128 in BM15PT, 120 in GP115PT, GP116BL, 112 in GP70CI, 104 in GP117PT, 96 in GP70CH, 88 in GP119BL, 80 in BM20PT, GP70HY, 72 in BM13WH, GP121PT, 64 in GP116WH, GP119WH, 56 in BM18BL, 40 in BM08PT, GP120PT, 32 in GP59MV, 16 in GP70SK and 8 in BM07LI. Total 1392 Diamonds.

Binding Cut 10 strips 2½in (6.5cm) across the width of the fabric in BM13BL.

Backing Cut 2 pieces 40in x 103in (101.5cm x 261.5cm) and 1 piece 24in x 103in (61cm x 261.5cm) in backing fabric.

MAKING THE QUILT
Using a ¼in (6mm) seam allowance throughout and referring to the quilt assembly diagram for fabric placement, piece the diamonds into rows as shown in the segment assembly diagram (the rows are generous as the edges will be trimmed later). Join the rows to form 2 segments. Join the 2 segments as shown to form a quarter of the quilt. Make 4 quarters and join to make the quilt as shown in the quilt assembly diagram.

Mark a line onto the quilt with a washable marker or masking tape as shown in the quilt assembly diagram.

SEGMENT ASSEMBLY DIAGRAM

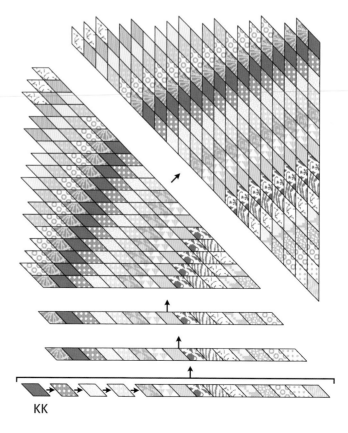

KK

QUILT ASSEMBLY DIAGRAM

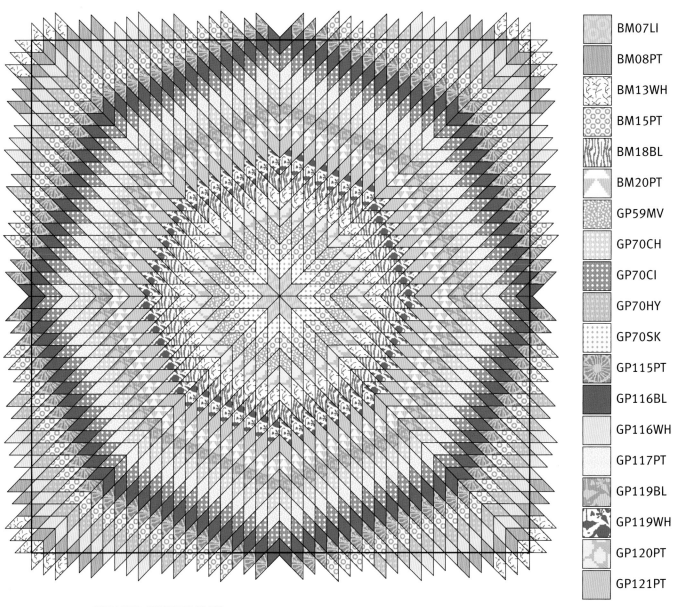

	BM07LI
	BM08PT
	BM13WH
	BM15PT
	BM18BL
	BM20PT
	GP59MV
	GP70CH
	GP70CI
	GP70HY
	GP70SK
	GP115PT
	GP116BL
	GP116WH
	GP117PT
	GP119BL
	GP119WH
	GP120PT
	GP121PT

TRIMMED QUILT DIAGRAM

At this stage trim the quilt edge about 1 inch (2.5cm) outside the marked line – this makes handling the quilt easier for layering and basting. Don't worry if there are a few gaps in the edge as final trimming will take place after the quilting is completed. The trimmed quilt diagram shows how the quilt will look after quilting and final trimming.

FINISHING THE QUILT

Press the quilt top. Seam the backing pieces using a ¼in (6mm) seam allowance to form a piece approx. 103in x 103in (261.5cm x 261.5cm). Layer the quilt top, batting and backing and baste together (see page 140). Using toning machine quilting thread either stitch in the ditch in all the seams or free motion quilt in an all over 'twirly' pattern. Trim the quilt edges leaving a ¼in (6mm) seam allowance outside the marked line and attach the binding (see page 141).

earthy big bang ***

Kaffe Fassett

This version of the Big Bang Quilt is made using the same method as Pastel Big Bang, this time using rich earthy colours.

SIZE OF QUILT
The finished quilt will measure approx. 95in x 95in (241.5cm x 241.5cm).

MATERIALS
Patchwork Fabrics
DAPPLE
Animal	BM05AM	¾yd (70cm)

STRAWS
Orange	BM08OR	¼yd (25cm)
Red	BM08RD	1⅛yd (1m)

BABBLE
Mist	BM13MI	¾yd (70cm)
Ochre	BM13OC	⅜yd (35cm)

RINGS
Beige	BM15BE	¾yd (70cm)
Olive	BM15OV	1¼yd (1.15m)

PAPERWEIGHT
Algae	GP20AL	1¼yd (1.15m)

GUINEA FLOWER
Brown	GP59BR	⅞yd (80cm)
Yellow	GP59YE	¾yd (70cm)

SPOT
Grey	GP70GY	1⅛yd (1m)

ASIAN CIRCLES
Turquoise	GP89TQ	⅝yd (60cm)

PLINK
Rust	GP109RU	⅛yd (15cm)

COGS
Dusty	GP110DU	1⅛yd (1m)

LINE DANCE
Lavender	GP116LV	1⅛yd (1m)

FOLK ART
Red	GP119RD	1¼yd (1.15m)

MAP
Brown	GP120BR	1yd (90cm)

KITE TAILS
Mauve	GP122MV	⅜yd (35cm)

Backing Fabric 9⅛yd (8.4m)
We suggest these fabrics for backing
LINE DANCE Lavender, GP116LV
GUINEA FLOWER Yellow, GP59YE
SPOT Grey, GP70GY

Binding Fabric
STRAWS
Red	BM08RD	1yd (90cm)

Batting
103in x 103in (261.5cm x 261.5cm)

Quilting threads
Toning machine quilting thread

Templates
See Pastel Big Bang.

CUTTING OUT
Template KK Cut 2¾in (7cm) strips across the width of the fabric. Each strip will give you 9 diamonds per full width. Cut 120 in BM15OV, GP20AL, 112 in GP119RD, 104 in BM08RD, GP70GY, GP110DU, GP116LV, 96 in GP120BR, 88 in GP59BR, 80 in BM05AM, BM15BE, 72 in BM13MI, GP59YE, 56 in GP89TQ, 32 in BM13OC, 24 in GP122MV, 16 in BM08OR and 8 in GP109RU. Total 1392 Diamonds.

Binding Cut 11yd (10m) of 2½in (6.5cm) wide bias binding in BM08RD.

Backing Cut 2 pieces 40in x 103in (101.5cm x 261.5cm) and 1 piece 24in x 103in (61cm x 261.5cm) in backing fabric.

MAKING THE QUILT
See Pastel Big Bang Instructions.

FINISHING THE QUILT
See Pastel Big Bang Instructions.

SEGMENT ASSEMBLY DIAGRAM

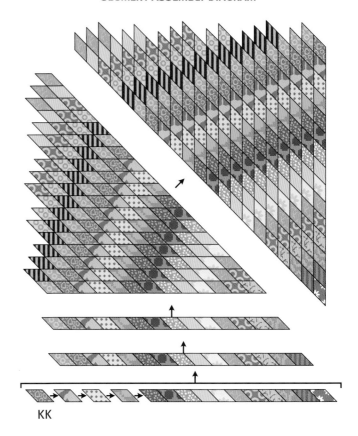

KK

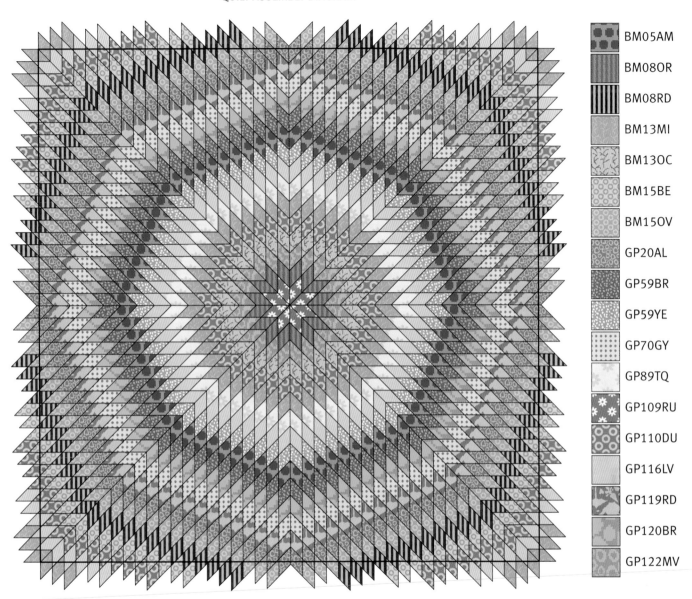

BM05AM	
BM08OR	
BM08RD	
BM13MI	
BM13OC	
BM15BE	
BM15OV	
GP20AL	
GP59BR	
GP59YE	
GP70GY	
GP89TQ	
GP109RU	
GP110DU	
GP116LV	
GP119RD	
GP120BR	
GP122MV	

green star bouquet ***

Kaffe Fassett

The main blocks which make up the quilt centre finish to 13in (33cm) and are made using 3 patch shapes, a large square (cut to size) a diamond (Template GG) and a lozenge shape (Template FF). The blocks are straight set into rows and where the blocks intersect a pretty star pattern is seen. The quilt centre is surrounded with a border pieced from 'Square in a Square' blocks which finish to 5in (12.75cm). These blocks are made using a square (Template JJ) and a triangle (Template HH). The border also has corner posts which are cut to size.

SIZE OF QUILT
The finished quilt will measure approx. 75in x 75in (190.5cm x 190.5cm).

MATERIALS
Patchwork and Border Fabrics
BABBLE
Mist	BM13MI	¼yd (25cm)

GUINEA FLOWER
Pink	GP59PK	¼yd (25cm)

SPOT
Green	GP70GN	¾yd (70cm)
Periwinkle	GP70PE	⅜yd (35cm)
Sapphire	GP70SP	¾yd (70cm)

ABORIGINAL DOTS
Delft	GP71DF	¼yd (25cm)
Periwinkle	GP71PE	¼yd (25cm)

ASIAN CIRCLES
Dark	GP89DK	⅜yd (35cm)
Green	GP89GN	⅜yd (35cm)
Turquoise	GP89TQ	⅜yd (35cm)

BIG BLOOMS
Emerald	GP91EM	⅜yd (35cm)

PLINK
Magenta	GP109MG	¼yd (25cm)

COLEUS
Turquoise	PJ30TQ	⅜yd (35cm)

RAMBLING ROSE
Violet	PJ34VI	½yd (45cm)

VARIEGATED IVY
Taupe	PJ36TA	½yd (45cm)

SHELL MONTAGE
Aqua	PJ37AQ	½yd (45cm)

PRIMULA
Sky	PJ42SK	½yd (45cm)

BEGONIA COLUMNS
Blue	PJ44BL	½yd (45cm)

SHOT COTTON
Cactus	SC90	¾yd (70cm)
Eucalyptus	SC92	¾yd (70cm)

Backing Fabric 5⅜yd (4.9m)
We suggest these fabrics for backing
BEGONIA COLUMNS Blue, PJ44BL
SHELL MONTAGE Aqua, PJ37AQ
BIG BLOOMS Emerald, GP91EM

Binding
GUINEA FLOWER
Pink	GP59PK	⅝yd (60cm)

Batting
83in x 83in (211cm x 211cm).

Quilting thread
Toning machine quilting thread and grey perlé embroidery thread.

Templates

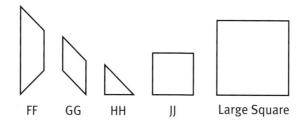

FF   GG   HH   JJ   Large Square

CUTTING OUT
Cut the fabric in the order stated to prevent waste.

Large Square Cut 9½in (24.25cm) strips across the width of the fabric. Each strip will give you 4 patches per full width. Cut 9½in (24.25cm) squares, cut 3 in PJ34VI. PJ36TA, PJ37AQ, PJ42SK, PJ44BL, 2 in GP89DK, GP89GN, GP89TQ, GP91EM and PJ30TQ. Total 25 Squares.

Border Corner Posts Cut 4 x 5½in (14cm) squares in GP89DK.

Template FF Cut 2½in (6.25cm) strips across the width of the fabric. Each strip will give you 6 patches per full width. Cut 50 in SC90 and SC92. Total 100 Lozenges.

Template GG Cut 2½in (6.25cm) strips across the width of the fabric. Each strip will give you 10 patches per full width. Cut 31 in GP70PE, 28 in GP70GN, 26 in BM13MI, GP70SP, 25 in GP71PE, 24 in GP59PK, 20 in GP71DF and GP109MG. Total 200 Diamonds.

Template HH Cut 3⅜in (8.5cm) strips across the width of the fabric. Each strip will give you 22 patches per full width. Cut 104 in GP70GN and GP70SP. Total 208 Triangles.

Template JJ Cut 4in (10.25cm) strips across the width of the fabric. Each strip will give you 10 patches per width. Cut 12 in PJ34VI, 11 in PJ37AQ, 10 in PJ36TA, 8 in PJ42SK, 6 in PJ44BL and 5 in GP91EM. Total 52 Squares.

Binding Cut 8 strips 2½in (6.5cm) wide across the width of the fabric in GP59PK.

Backing Cut 2 pieces 40in x 83in (101.5cm x 211cm), 2 pieces 40in x 4in (101.5cm x 10.25cm) and 1 piece 4in x 4in (10.25cm x 10.25cm) in backing fabric. For a quirky look to the backing you could cut the 4in square from a different fabric and piece the backing with the contrasting square in the centre.

MAKING THE MAIN BLOCKS
Use a ¼in (6mm) seam allowance throughout. Refer to the quilt assembly diagram for fabric placement. For the main blocks the inset seam method is used (see Patchwork Know How on page 139). Make 25 blocks following the main block assembly diagrams.

MAKING THE BORDER BLOCKS
Refer to the quilt assembly diagram for fabric placement. Piece a total of 52 border blocks following border block assembly diagrams e and f. The finished border block can be seen in diagram g.

MAKING THE QUILT

Join the main blocks into 5 rows of 5 blocks, then join the rows to form the quilt centre. Stitch the border blocks into 4 rows of 13 blocks. Add a row to each side of the quilt centre, then join a border corner post to each end of the remaining 2 rows. Finally add these to the top and bottom of the quilt centre.

FINISHING THE QUILT

Press the quilt top. Seam the backing pieces using a ¼in (6mm) seam allowance to form a piece approx. 83in x 83in (211cm x 211cm). Layer the quilt top, batting and backing and baste together (see page 140). Using toning machine quilting thread, quilt in the ditch in all the seams. On the large squares hand quilt squares 1½in (3.75cm) from the seam using grey perlé embroidery thread. Trim the quilt edges and attach the binding (see page 141).

MAIN BLOCK ASSEMBLY DIAGRAMS

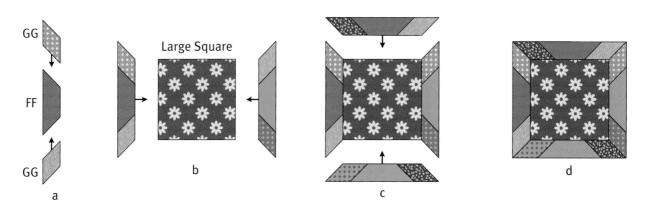

a   b   c   d

Kaffe says:

Inset seams are fiddly to do, but get much easier with a little practice, we have found it is better to stitch all the blocks to this stage and then complete all the inset seaming together. Therefore for all the main blocks follow block assembly diagrams a and b. Get all the blocks to this stage, then using the inset seam method complete the blocks as shown in block assembly diagram c. The finished block can be seen in diagram d.

BORDER BLOCK ASSEMBLY DIAGRAMS

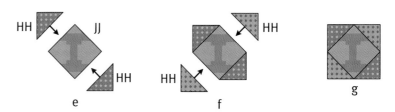

e   f   g

QUILT ASSEMBLY DIAGRAM

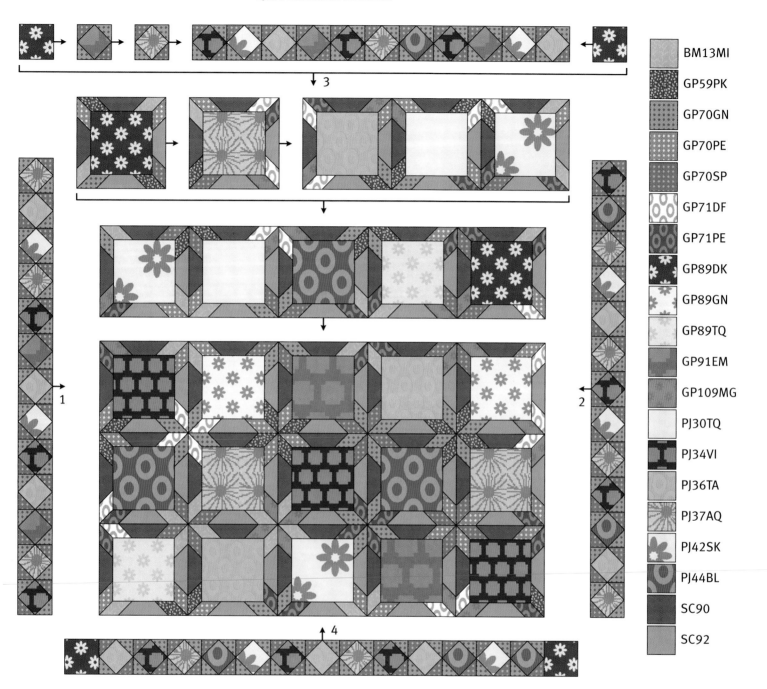

	BM13MI
	GP59PK
	GP70GN
	GP70PE
	GP70SP
	GP71DF
	GP71PE
	GP89DK
	GP89GN
	GP89TQ
	GP91EM
	GP109MG
	PJ30TQ
	PJ34VI
	PJ36TA
	PJ37AQ
	PJ42SK
	PJ44BL
	SC90
	SC92

rich chevrons **

Kaffe Fassett

A triangle (Template LL) is pieced into square blocks to make up the centre of this quilt. The stripe direction is the key to this pattern and a design wall is very helpful when laying out the triangles. The blocks are pieced into diagonal rows with the same triangle patch shape used to fill the ends of the rows, this time fussy cut to align the stripes with the long side of the triangles. The extreme corners of the quilt are completed using a second triangle (Template MM).

SIZE OF QUILT
The finished quilt will measure approx. 84½in x 65½in (214.5cm x 166.5cm).

MATERIALS
Patchwork Fabrics
STRAWS

Grey	BM08GY	¼yd (25cm)
Lime	BM08LM	¼yd (25cm)
Orange	BM08OR	1yd (90cm)
Pink	BM08PK	¼yd (25cm)

WRINKLE

Brown	BM18BR	¼yd (25cm)

MARQUEE

Bright	GP121BT	Fussy cut, see below*

WOVEN ALTERNATING STRIPE

Orange	WAS OR	½yd (45cm)
Olive	WAS OV	¼yd (25cm)
Red	WAS RD	¼yd (25cm)
Yellow	WAS YE	½yd (45cm)

WOVEN BROAD STRIPE

Dark	WBS DK	¼yd (25cm)
Earth	WBS ER	¼yd (25cm)
Sunset	WBS SS	½yd (45cm)
Red	WBS RD	¼yd (25cm)
Yellow	WBS YE	½yd (45cm)

WOVEN CATERPILLAR STRIPE

Earth	WCS ER	¼yd (25cm)
Tomato	WCS TM	½ yd (45cm)
Yellow	WCS YE	½yd (45cm)

WOVEN EXOTIC STRIPE

Dark	WES DK	¼yd (25cm)
Dusk	WES DU	¼yd (25cm)
Earth	WES ER	¼yd (25cm)
Purple	WES PU	¼yd (25cm)
Warm	WES WM	½yd (45cm)

WOVEN NARROW STRIPE

Dark	WNS DK	¼yd (25cm)
Earth	WNS ER	¼yd (25cm)
Red	WNS RD	½yd (45cm)
Yellow	WNS YE	½yd (45cm)

*The MARQUEE Bright, GP121BT fabric is printed in 6 sections each with a different colour combination. For this quilt you will only use the orange/magenta, yellow/red and purple/ochre sections. You will need 3 sections each of orange/magenta and yellow/red and 2 sections of purple/ochre. This means buying a quantity between 1⅜yd and 1¾yd (1.25m and 1.6m). There will be plenty of unused fabric, we suggest making bunting flags with the surplus.

Backing Fabric 5½yd (5m)
We suggest these fabrics for backing
MAP Brown, GP120BR
WOVEN EXOTIC STRIPE Earth, WES ER or Warm WES WM

Binding Fabric
STRAWS

Orange	BM08OR	¾yd (70cm)

Batting
92in x 73in (233.5cm x 185.5cm)

Quilting thread
Toning machine quilting thread.

Templates

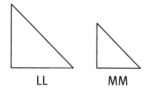

LL   MM

CUTTING OUT
IMPORTANT INFORMATION. Please read carefully before cutting any fabrics. For the Woven Stripe fabrics cutting is easy as they are fully reversible, cut all the triangles as shown in cutting and block assembly diagram a, from top right to bottom left (stripes vertical). This gives the correct stripe orientation for the left side of the pieced block as shown in diagram c. If you need a triangle for the right side of a block just flip one over. For the printed fabrics (Straws, Wrinkle and Marquee) the triangles must be cut to suit the position in the block. Cut as shown in diagram a for the left side of the block and as shown in diagram b, from top left to bottom right (stripes vertical) for the right side of the block. The edge and corner triangles are fussy cut, details below. Cut the fabric in the order stated to prevent waste.

Quilt Centre
Template LL Cut 7½in (19cm) strips across the width of the fabric, each strip will give 10 triangles per full width. Cut 14 in GP121BT (5 in Orange/Magenta, 5 in Yellow/Red and 4 in Purple/Ochre stripes), 14 in WAS OR, WES WM, WNS RD, WNS YE, 13 in WBS SS, WBS YE, 12 in WAS YE, WCS TM, WCS YE, 10 in WAS OV, WBS RD, 8 in BM08PK, WAS RD, WCS ER, WES DK, WES ER, 6 in WBS DK, WES DU, 4 in BM18BR, WNS ER, 2 in BM08GY, BM08LM, WBS ER, WES PU and WNS DK. Total 222 Triangles.

Edge and Corner Triangles fabric
BM08OR
Template MM Cut a 5½in (14cm) strip across the width of the fabric, cut 2 squares 5½in x 5½in (14cm x 14cm). Ensuring that the stripes will run correctly at the quilt corners, cut each square diagonally to form 2 triangles using the template as a guide. Total 4 Triangles.
Template LL From the remaining fabric cut 5⅜in (13.75cm) strips down the length of the fabric. With the stripes aligned with the long side of the template cut 28 triangles.

Binding Cut 8⅝yd (7.9m) of 2½in (6.5cm) wide bias binding in BM08OR.

Backing Cut 1 piece 40in x 92in (101.5cm x 233.5cm) and 1 piece 34in x 92in (86.5cm x 233.5cm) in backing fabric.

MAKING THE QUILT
Use ¼in (6mm) seam allowance throughout. Refer to the quilt assembly diagram and photograph for fabric placement. Lay out the quilt centre triangles on a design wall and ensure all the stripes are in the correct orientation. Piece a total of 111 blocks as shown in cutting and block assembly diagram c, the finished block is shown in diagram d. Again lay out the pieced blocks on the design wall to check orientation and fill in the edges of the quilt with the BM08OR triangles, then separate into diagonal rows as shown in the quilt assembly diagram.

CUTTING AND BLOCK ASSEMBLY DIAGRAMS

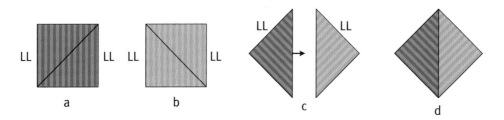

a   b   c   d

QUILT ASSEMBLY DIAGRAM

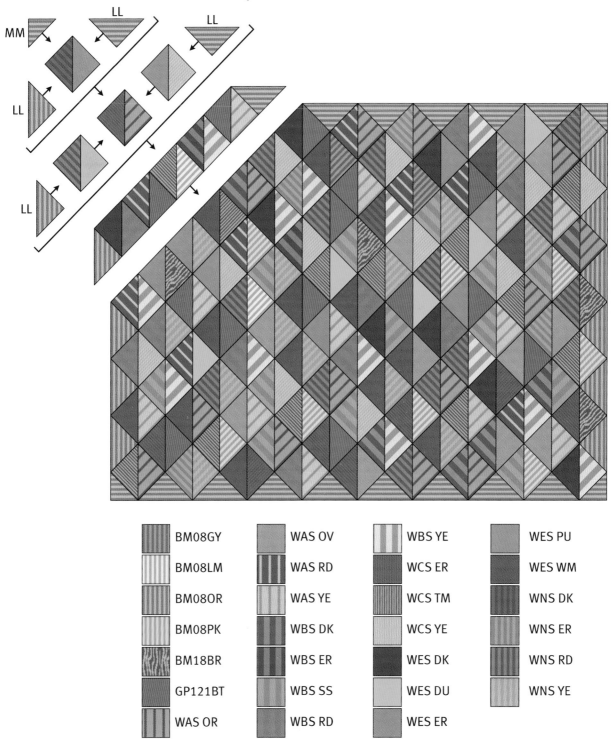

BM08GY	WAS OV	WBS YE	WES PU
BM08LM	WAS RD	WCS ER	WES WM
BM08OR	WAS YE	WCS TM	WNS DK
BM08PK	WBS DK	WCS YE	WNS ER
BM18BR	WBS ER	WES DK	WNS RD
GP121BT	WBS SS	WES DU	WNS YE
WAS OR	WBS RD	WES ER	

Join the blocks and edge triangles into rows, then join the rows to form the quilt centre. Finally add the corner triangles to complete the quilt.

FINISHING THE QUILT

Press the quilt top. Seam the backing pieces using a ¼in (6mm) seam allowance to form a piece approx. 92in x 73in (233.5cm x 185.5cm). Layer the quilt top, batting and backing and baste together (see page 140). Using toning machine quilting thread quilt all the seams in the ditch. Also quilt the blocks, edge triangles and corner triangles as shown in the quilting diagram. Trim the quilt edges and attach the binding (see page 141).

QUILTING DIAGRAM

marquee chevrons **

Kaffe Fassett

This second version of Kaffe's chevrons quilt is constructed in the same way as Rich Chevrons, but is larger. This time colour is the key to the design. We have allowed generous quantities of the 3 Marquee fabrics as they are fussy cut. These fabrics are printed in 6 sections each with a different colour combination.

SIZE OF QUILT
The finished quilt will measure approx. 84½in x 84½in (214.5cm x 214.5cm).

MATERIALS
Patchwork Fabrics
WRINKLE

Blue	BM18BL	1¼yd (1.15m)

MARQUEE

Bright	GP121BT	5¾yd (5.25m)
Contrast	GP121CO	4½yd (4.1m)
Pastel	GP121PT	4½yd (4.1m)

Backing Fabric 6⅝yd (6.1m)
We suggest these fabrics for backing
MARQUEE Pastel, GP121PT or Bright, GP121BT

Binding Fabric
WRINKLE

Blue	BM18BL	⅞yd (80cm)

Batting
92in x 92in (233.5cm x 233.5cm)

Quilting thread
White machine quilting thread.

Templates
See Rich Chevrons.

CUTTING OUT
IMPORTANT INFORMATION. Please read carefully before cutting any fabrics. The triangles must be cut to suit the position in the block. We suggest leaving the fabrics as squares until you are ready to position them onto a design wall, then cut the squares diagonally to suit the position in the blocks. Cut as shown in Rich Chevrons cutting and block assembly diagram a or b depending on the stripe direction required. The edge and corner triangles are fussy cut, details below. Cut the fabric in the order stated to prevent waste.

Quilt Centre
Template LL Cut 7½in (19cm) strips across the width of the fabric, each strip will give 10 triangles per full width. Cut 140 in GP121BT (32 in Purple/Ochre, 31 in Orange/Magenta, 28 in Yellow/Red, 26 in Purple/Turquoise, 16 in Powder Blue/Shocking Pink and 7 in Pink/Emerald stripes), 82 in GP121PT (17 in White/Pale Blue, Pale Pink/Gold, 15 in Lemon/Lavender, Lemon/Pink, 11 in Buff/Orange and 7 in Pale Pink/Green), 68 in GP121CO (17 in White/Cobalt, 15 in White/Deep Pink, 12 in White/Green, 11 in White/Black, 7 in White/Purple and 6 in White/Brown) Total 290 Triangles.

Edge and Corner Triangles fabric BM18BL
Template MM Cut a 5½in (14cm) strip across the width of the fabric, cut 2 squares 5½in x 5½in (14cm x 14cm). Ensuring that the stripes will run correctly at the quilt corners, cut each square diagonally to form 2 triangles using the template as a guide. Total 4 Triangles.
Template LL From the remaining fabric cut 5⅜in (13.75cm) strips down the length of the fabric. With the stripes aligned with the long side of the template cut 32 triangles.

Binding Cut 9¾yd (8.9m) of 2½in (6.5cm) wide bias binding in BM18BL.

Backing Cut 2 pieces 40in x 92in (101.5cm x 233.5cm), 2 pieces 40in x 13in (101.5cm x 33cm) and 1 piece 13in x 13in (33cm x 33cm) in backing fabric.

MAKING THE QUILT
Use ¼in (6mm) seam allowance throughout. Refer to the quilt assembly diagram and photograph for fabric placement. Lay out the quilt centre triangles on a design wall and ensure all the stripes are in the correct orientation. Piece a total of 145 blocks as shown in Rich Chevrons cutting and block assembly diagram c, the finished block is shown in diagram d (note that the stripe directions may vary for this version). Again lay out the pieced blocks on the design wall to check orientation and fill in the edges of the quilt with the BM18BL triangles, then separate into diagonal rows as shown in the quilt assembly diagram. Join the blocks and edge triangles into rows, then join the rows to form the quilt centre. Finally add the corner triangles to complete the quilt.

FINISHING THE QUILT
Press the quilt top. Seam the backing pieces using a ¼in (6mm) seam allowance to form a piece approx. 92in x 92in (233.5cm x 233.5cm). Layer the quilt top, batting and backing and baste together (see page 140). Using white machine quilting thread quilt all the seams in the ditch. Also quilt the blocks following the stripes and the edge triangles following the wavy lines of the fabric. Trim the quilt edges and attach the binding (see page 141).

Kaffe says:
Because it is cut on the bias, the long edge of the triangle is slightly stretchy. To make sure each block makes a perfect square, pin each pair of triangles together carefully before stitching.

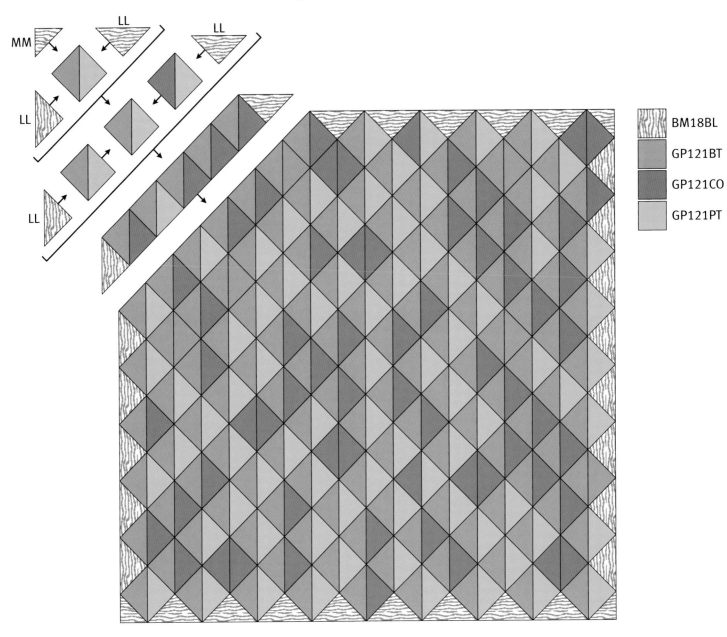

sunshine stars ★★

Kaffe Fassett

Traditional sawtooth stars are easy and fun to make with 2 squares (Template Y and Z) and 1 triangle (Template H). The blocks finish to 11in (28cm) square and are set in straight rows to form the quilt centre. The quilt is finished with a simple border.

SIZE OF QUILT
The finished quilt will measure approx. 63in x 74in (160cm x 188cm).

MATERIALS
Patchwork and Border Fabrics
STRAWS
Pink	BM08PK	¼yd (25cm)

BABBLE
Yellow	BM13YE	¼yd (25cm)

AURORA
Yellow	BM21YE	¼yd (25cm)

CLOVER DOTS
Spice	BM23SI	¼yd (25cm)

PETRA
Lime	BM24LM	¼yd (25cm)

PLAID
Yellow	BM26YE	⅜yd (35cm)

ROPE
Yellow	BM28YE	¼yd (25cm)

PAPERWEIGHT
Yellow	GP20YE	¼yd (25cm)

ZINNIA
Pink	GP31PK	¼yd (25cm)

GUINEA FLOWER
Apricot	GP59AP	¼yd (25cm)
Gold	GP59GD	¼yd (25cm)
Turquoise	GP59TQ	¼yd (25cm)

PAISLEY JUNGLE
Lime	GP60LM	⅜yd (35cm)

SPOT
Gold	GP70GD	⅜yd (35cm)
Lavender	GP70LV	¼yd (25cm)
Paprika	GP70PP	¼yd (25cm)
Turquoise	GP70TQ	¼yd (25cm)

ABORIGINAL DOTS
Cantaloupe	GP71CA	¼yd (25cm)
Lilac	GP71LI	¼yd (25cm)
Lime	GP71LM	¼yd (25cm)

ASIAN CIRCLES
Yellow	GP89YE	¼yd (25cm)

LINE DANCE
Yellow	GP116YE	¼yd (25cm)

FIELD BOUQUET
Primrose	GP118PR	1 strip of panels

MAP
Red	GP120RD	¼yd (25cm)

SCALLOPS
Warm	PJ45WM	1¼yd (1.15m)

SHOT COTTON
Apple	SC39	⅜yd (35cm)
Lipstick	SC83	⅜yd (35cm)

WOVEN ALTERNATING STRIPE
Yellow	WAS YE	⅜yd (35cm)

Backing Fabric 4⅞yd (4.5m)
We suggest these fabrics for backing
MOONFLOWERS Yellow, PJ48YE
PAISLEY JUNGLE Lime, GP60LM
WOVEN ALTERNATING STRIPE Yellow, WAS YE

Binding
SPOT
Paprika	GP70PP	⅝yd (60cm)

Batting
71in x 82in (180.5cm x 208.5cm)

Quilting Thread
Toning machine quilting thread

Templates

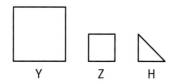
Y   Z   H

CUTTING OUT
Cut the patch shapes in the order specified, always keeping remaining fabric in the largest size possible.
Borders Cut 7 strips 4½in (11.5cm) across the width of the fabric, join as necessary and cut 2 strips 4½in x 74½in (11.5cm x 189.25cm) for the quilt sides and 2 strips 4½in x 55½in (11.5cm x 141cm) for the quilt top and bottom.
Template Y Cut 6in (15.25cm) squares. Cut 3 in GP60LM, GP118PR, 2 in BM21YE, BM26YE, BM28YE, GP20YE, GP31PK, GP59GD, GP89YE, GP116YE, GP120RD, PJ45WM, 1 in BM23SI, BM24LM, GP70GD and WAS YE.
Template H Cut 3⅝in (9.25cm) squares, cut each square in half diagonally to form 2 triangles using the template as a guide. Cut 32 in SC83, 24 in BM26YE, GP60LM, GP118PR, SC39, 16 in BM08PK, BM13YE, BM21YE, BM28YE, GP20YE, GP31PK, GP59AP, GP59GD, GP59TQ, GP70GD, GP70LV, GP70PP, GP70TQ, GP71CA, GP71LI, GP71LM, GP89YE, GP116YE, GP120RD, PJ45WM, WAS YE, 8 in BM23SI and BM24LM.
Template Z Cut 3¼in (8.25cm) squares. Cut 16 in SC83, 12 in SC39, 8 in BM08PK, BM13YE, GP59AP, GP59TQ, GP70LV, GP70PP, GP70TQ, GP71CA, GP71LI, GP71LM, 4 in BM26YE, GP70GD and WAS YE.

Binding Cut 8 strips 2½in (6.5cm) wide across the width of the fabric in GP70PP.

Backing Cut 1 piece 40in x 82in (101.5cm x 208.25cm) and 1 piece 32in x 82in (81.25cm x 208.25cm) in backing fabric.

MAKING THE BLOCKS
Use a ¼in (6mm) seam allowance throughout. Use the quilt assembly diagram as a guide to fabric placement. Make 30 blocks as shown in block assembly diagrams a and b, the finished block is shown in diagram c. Join the blocks into 6 rows of 5 blocks as shown in the quilt assembly diagram. Join the rows to form the quilt centre.

BLOCK ASSEMBLY DIAGRAMS

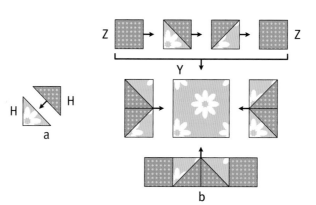

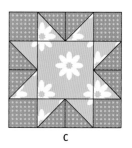

QUILT ASSEMBLY DIAGRAM

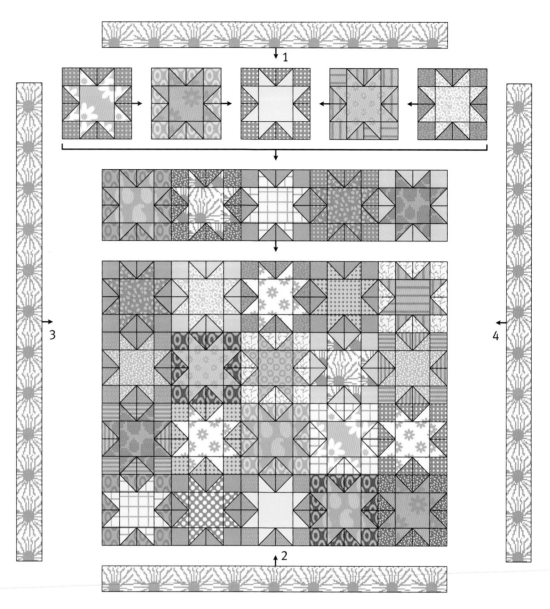

MAKING THE QUILT

Join the blocks into 6 rows of 5 blocks then join the rows to form the quilt centre.

Add the top and bottom, then the side borders as shown in the quilt assembly diagram to complete the quilt.

FINISHING THE QUILT

Press the quilt top. Seam the backing pieces using a ¼in (6mm) seam allowance to form a piece approx. 71in x 82in (180.5cm x 208.5cm). Layer the quilt top, batting and backing and baste together (see page 140). Using toning quilting thread, stitch in the ditch by hand or machine in all the seams. Trim the quilt edges and attach the binding (see page 141).

BM08PK	GP20YE	GP70LV	GP116YE
BM13YE	GP31PK	GP70PP	GP118PR
BM21YE	GP59AP	GP70TQ	GP120RD
BM23SI	GP59GD	GP71CA	PJ45WM
BM24LM	GP59TQ	GP71LI	SC39
BM26YE	GP60LM	GP71LM	SC83
BM28YE	GP70GD	GP89YE	WAS YE

garden chintz *

Kaffe Fassett

The centre of this quilt is a panel cut to size, surrounded by 2 simple borders. This section is then surrounded with traditional Snowball blocks, made from an octagon and four triangles, in this case it is made 'the easy way' by using a large square (Template O) and 4 small squares (Template P) for each block. The small squares are placed over the corners of the large squares and stitched diagonally. They are then trimmed and flipped back to replace the corners of the large square. The centre is then surrounded with simple border to complete the quilt.

SIZE OF QUILT
The finished quilt will measure approx.
75½in x 90½in (192cm x 230cm).

MATERIALS
Patchwork and Border Fabrics
LOTUS LEAF

Antique	GP29AN	⅜yd (35cm)
GUINEA FLOWER		
Yellow	GP59YE	2¼yd (2.1m)
SPOT		
Ice	GP70IC	⅜yd (35cm)
ASIAN CIRCLES		
Chartreuse	GP89CT	⅝yd (60cm)
BIG BLOOMS		
Brown	GP91BR	⅝yd (60cm)
FOLK ART		
Rust	GP119RU	1½yd (1.4m)
KITE TAILS		
Mauve	GP122MV	¾yd (70cm)
BEGONIA COLUMNS		
Brown	PJ44BR	⅝yd (60cm)
Green	PJ44GN	⅝yd (60cm)
SCALLOPS		
Green	PJ45GN	⅝yd (60cm)
Purple	PJ45PU	⅜yd (35cm)
LACY		
Brown	PJ46BR	⅝yd (60cm)
Cool	PJ46CL	⅝yd (60cm)
MIAMI		
Green	PJ47GN	¾yd (70cm)
MOON FLOWER		
Autumn	PJ48AT	⅜yd (35cm)
FLOATING MUMS		
Taupe	PJ49TA	⅜yd (35cm)

Backing Fabric 6½yd (6m)
We suggest these fabrics for backing
BEGONIA COLUMNS Brown, PJ44BR
SCALLOPS Green, PJ45GN
ASIAN CIRCLES Chartreuse, GP89CT

Binding
SPOT

Ice	GP70IC	¾yd (70cm)

Batting
84in x 99in (213cm x 251.5cm)

Quilting Thread
Toning machine quilting thread
Taupe hand quilting thread

Templates

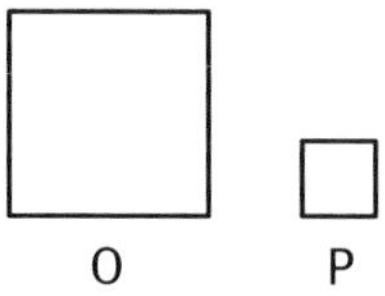

O   P

CUTTING OUT
Cut the fabric in the order stated to prevent waste.
Centre Panel Cut 1 rectangle 17in x 24½in (43.25cm x 62.25cm) in PJ47GN.
Border 1 Cut 2 strips 24½in x 2½in (62.25cm x 6.25cm) for the sides and 2 strips 21in x 2½in (53.5cm x 6.25cm) for the top and bottom in GP70IC.
Border 2 Cut 2 strips 28½in x 1½in (72.5cm x 3.75cm) for the sides and 2 strips 23in x 1½in (58.5cm x 3.75cm) for the top and bottom in GP119RU.
Border 3 Cut 9 strips 4½in (11.5cm) wide across the width of fabric in GP119RU. Join as necessary and cut 2 strips 4½in x 83in (11.5cm x 211cm) for the sides of the quilt and 2 strips 4½in x 76in (11.5cm x 193cm) for the top and bottom of the quilt.
Template O Cut 8in (20.25cm) strips across the width of the fabric. Each strip will give you 5 squares per full width. Cut 12 in GP122MV, 10 in PJ44BR, 8 in GP89CT, GP91BR, PJ45GN, PJ46BR, 6 in PJ44GN, PJ46CL, 5 in PJ48AT, 4 in GP29AN, PJ45PU, PJ47GN and PJ49TA. Total 87 Squares.
Template P Cut 2¾in (7cm) strips across the width of the fabric. Each strip will give you 14 squares per full width. Cut 348 in GP59YE.

Kaffe says:
For this quilt it is important to place the blocks with a strong directional print (such as Begonia Columns, Kite Tails and Scallops) so that the pattern runs vertically down the quilt.

QUILT CENTRE ASSEMBLY DIAGRAM

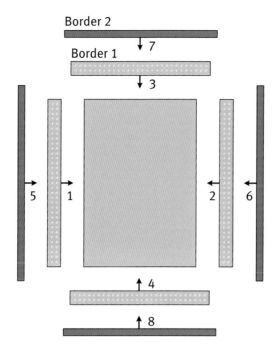

BLOCK ASSEMBLY DIAGRAMS

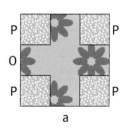

a   b   c

Binding Cut 9 strips 2½in (6.5cm) across the width of the fabric in GP70IC.

Backing Cut 2 pieces 40in x 99in (101.5cm x 251.5cm), 2 pieces 40in x 5in (101.5cm x 12.75cm) and 1 piece 20in x 5in (50.75cm x 12.75cm) in backing fabric.

MAKING THE CENTRE PANEL
Use a ¼in (6mm) seam allowance throughout. Take the centre panel of PJ47GN fabric and join a Border 1 side to each side. Then join the Border 1 top and bottom to the top and bottom of the centre panel. Press carefully and join border 2 in the same way as shown in the quilt centre assembly diagram.

MAKING THE SNOWBALL BLOCKS
To make the Snowball blocks take one large square (template O) and four small squares (template P). Place one small square, right sides together onto each corner of the large square, matching the edges carefully as shown in block assembly diagram a. Stitch diagonally across the small squares as shown in diagram b. Trim the corners to a ¼in (6mm) seam allowance and press the corners out (diagram c). Make 87 blocks.

MAKING THE QUILT
Use a ¼in (6mm) seam allowance throughout. Lay out all the blocks as shown in the quilt assembly diagram. Piece the snowball blocks into sections as shown and join to the centre panel.

Finally add border 3, first the sides, then the top and bottom as shown in the quilt assembly diagram.

FINISHING THE QUILT
Press the quilt top. Seam the backing pieces using a ¼in (6mm) seam allowance to form a piece approx 84in x 99in (213cm x 251.5cm). Layer the quilt top, batting and backing and baste together (see page 140). Using toning machine quilting thread quilt in the ditch around the blocks and in the border seams, free motion quilt the centre panel following the foliage in the fabric print, quilt the outer border in the same way. On the centre of each snowball block hand quilt a 4¾in (12cm) diameter circle, using taupe thread. Trim the quilt edges and attach the binding (see page 141).

QUILT ASSEMBLY DIAGRAM

Border 3

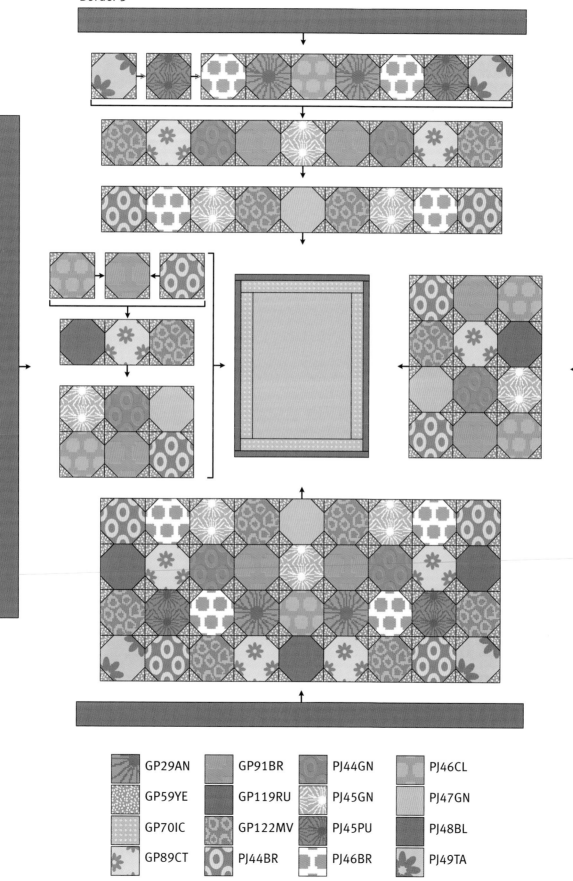

GP29AN	GP91BR	PJ44GN	PJ46CL
GP59YE	GP119RU	PJ45GN	PJ47GN
GP70IC	GP122MV	PJ45PU	PJ48BL
GP89CT	PJ44BR	PJ46BR	PJ49TA

dotty all season garden **

Mary Mashuta

The quilt centre is made from four zigzag strips pieced from 2 triangle patch shapes (Templates A and B). The triangles which form the zigzags are cut from Kaffe's new Woven Alternating Stripe fabrics, which Mary, the stripe expert, fussy cut with the stripes running in alternating directions. The pieced strips are alternated with sections of floral fabric cut from 3 colourways of the same print. The quilt is finished by a border with corner posts.

SIZE OF QUILT
The finished quilt will measure approx. 58in x 64in (147.5cm x 162.5cm).

MATERIALS
Patchwork Fabrics
LOTUS LEAF

Antique	GP29AN	⅝yd (60cm)
Green	GP29GN	⅝yd (60cm)
Jade	GP29JA	⅝yd (60cm)

SPOT

Burgundy	GP70BG	¼yd (25cm)
Gold	GP70GD	¼yd (25cm)
Magenta	GP70 MG	¼yd (25cm)
Yellow	GP70YE	¼yd (25cm)

WOVEN ALTERNATING STRIPE

Orange	WAS OR	½yd (45cm)
Red	WAS RD	½yd (45cm)
Teal	WAS TE	½yd (45cm)
Yellow	WAS YE	½yd (45cm)

Border Fabrics
RINGS

| Green | BM15GN | ¼yd (25cm) |

KITE TAILS

| Black | GP122BK | ½yd (45cm) |
| Mauve | GP122MV | ½yd (45cm) |

Backing Fabric 3⅞yd (3.6m)
We suggest these fabrics for backing
AURORA   Green BM21GN
WOVEN ALTERNATING STRIPE
Orange WAS OR
LOTUS LEAF   Jade GP29JA

Binding
SHOT COTTON

| Grape | SC47 | ⅝yd (60cm) |

Batting
66in x 72in (167.5cm x 183cm)

Quilting thread
Toning machine quilting thread
Contrasting machine quilting thread
Optional, perlé embroidery thread for borders

Templates

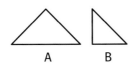

A   B

CUTTING OUT
IMPORTANT INFORMATION. Please read carefully before cutting the stripe fabric triangles.
1 The grain placement and stripe pattern placement are important graphically and technically. (Accurate grain placement keeps fabric from stretching along the longest edge when sewing in strips and joining to floral strips later.)
2 Some pieces will need to be 'fussy' cut to read correctly visually.
3 You can only cut 1 layer of the stripe fabric at a time if stripes are to remain exactly on grain and be visually correct.
4 You may decide to cut a few extra stripe triangles so you can have more options in arranging them, a little extra yardage has been allowed for this.

Template B SPOT FABRICS Cut a 3⅞in (10cm) strip across the width of the fabric. Cut 2 in GP70BG, GP70GD, GP70MG and GP70YE. Total 8 triangles. Reserve the leftover strip and trim for template A.

Template A SPOT FABRICS Cut 3⅝in (9.25cm) strips across the width of the fabric. Align the template with the long side along the cut edge of the strip, this will ensure the long side of the triangles will not have a bias edge. Each strip will give you 9 patches per full width. Cut 17 in GP70BG, GP70GD, GP70MG and GP70YE. Total 68 triangles.

Template A STRIPE FABRICS Carefully true up the stripe fabrics so that the stripes are exactly perpendicular to the cut edge. From each of the striped fabrics cut 1 strip 3⅝in (9.25cm) across the width of the fabric. From this 'fussy' cut 9 triangles in WAS OR, WAS RD, WAS TE and WAS YE as shown in cutting diagram 1. Total 36 triangles.
From the remaining STRIPE FABRICS Fussy cut 8 Template A triangles in WAS OR, WAS RD, WAS TE and WAS YE along the length of the stripes, as shown in cutting diagram 2. Total 32 triangles.

Template B STRIPE FABRICS Cut 2 in WAS OR, WAS RD, WAS TE and WAS YE. Total 8 triangles.

CUTTING DIAGRAM 2

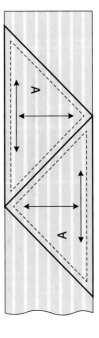

CUTTING DIAGRAM 1

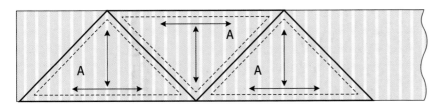

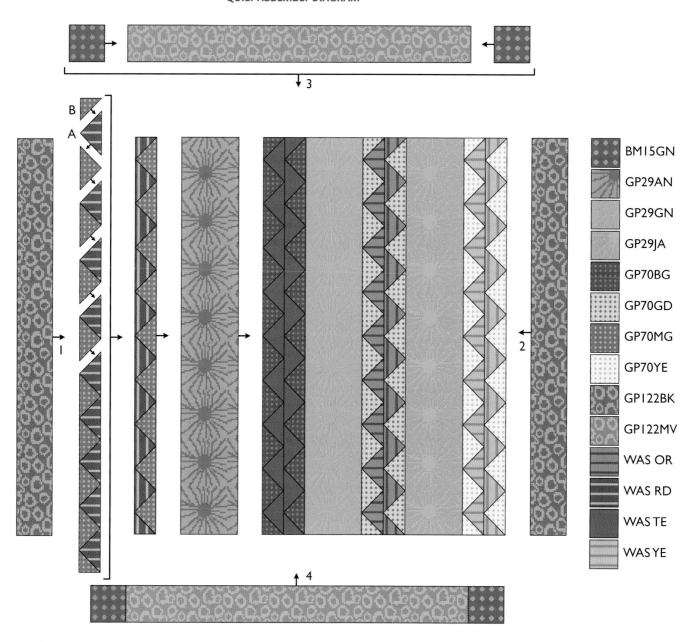

Floral Strips From each of the floral fabrics cut 2 strips 8½in (21.5cm) across the width of the fabric, join as necessary and cut 1 strip 8½in x 54½in (21.5cm x 138.5cm) from GP29AN, GP29GN and GP29JA.

Border Cut 3 strips 5½in (14cm) across the width of the fabric in GP122BK, join as necessary and cut 2 borders 5½in x 54½in (14cm x 138.5cm) for the quilt sides. Cut 3 strips 5½in (14cm) across the width of the fabric in GP112MV, join as necessary and cut 2 borders 5½in x

48½in (14cm x 123.25cm) for the quilt top and bottom.

Border Corner Posts Cut 4 squares 5½in x 5½in (14cm x 14cm) in BM15GN.

Binding Cut 6 strips 2½in (6.5cm) across width of the fabric in SC47.

Backing Cut 1 piece 40in x 66in (101.5cm x 167.5cm) and 1 piece 33in x 66in (84cm x 167.5cm) in backing fabric.

MAKING THE ZIGZAG STRIPS
Use a ¼in (6mm) seam allowance throughout. Arrange all the stripe and spot triangles in rows as shown in the quilt assembly diagram. You may want to fine tune the placement of the triangles before sewing. Join the triangles 2 at a time being careful not to stretch the bias edges. You may find it helpful to place 3 pins across each seam, gently place your finger on the pin to help guide it through your machine. Join the triangles to form rows and press the seams open. Join two strips of joined triangles being careful

to create zigzag patterns. (Mark the middle of each triangle with a pin to use as a guide in lining up the rows.) Press the seam towards the triangles with the stripe along the long side.

MAKING THE QUILT

Arrange the floral and pieced strips alternately as shown in the quilt assembly diagram join to form the quilt centre. Add the side borders, join a corner post to each end of the top and bottom borders and add them to the quilt centre to complete the quilt.

FINISHING THE QUILT

Press the quilt top. Seam the backing pieces using a ¼in (6mm) seam allowance to form a piece approx. 66in x 72in (167.5cm x 183cm). Layer the quilt top, batting and backing and baste together (see page 140). Using toning machine quilting thread quilt all the vertical and horizontal seams in the ditch. Quilt the zigzag strips as shown in the quilting diagram, the areas filled grey in the diagram are meander quilted following the fabric designs. Trim the quilt edges and attach the binding (see page 141).

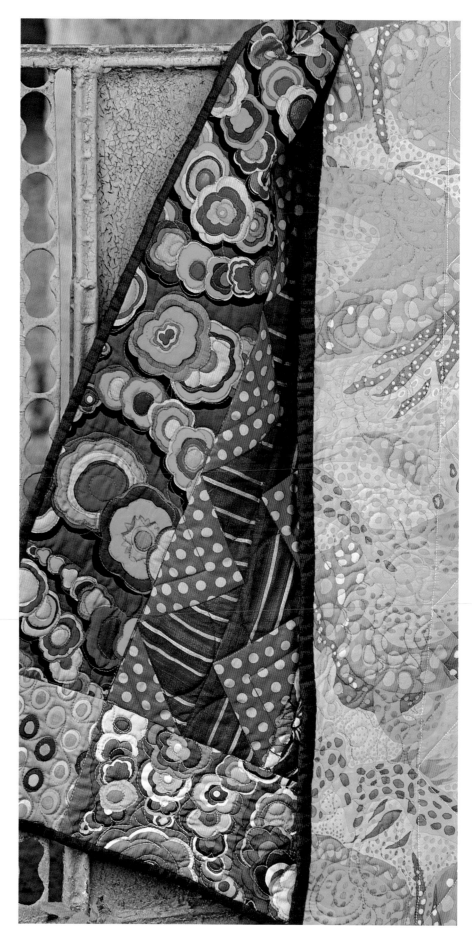

summer chelsea **

Pauline Smith

The background of this pretty quilt is pieced from a selection of rectangles, cut to size. These are pieced into 3 columns and joined to form the quilt centre. Simple hand appliqué is then added to the background. We have provided example templates for the flower, leaf and small vase shapes as a starting point, vary them as you please. The larger vase is a simple rectangle, cut to size. The flower stems are also cut to size. The quilt is finished with a border with corner posts cut to size.

SIZE OF QUILT
The finished quilt will measure approx.
45¾in x 51¾in (116.25cm x 131.5cm).

MATERIALS
Patchwork and Border Fabrics
RINGS
Beige   BM15BE   ⅜yd (35cm)
PAPERWEIGHT
Paprika   GP20PP   ⅜yd (35cm)
GUINEA FLOWER
Brown   GP59BR   ⅜yd (35cm)
ABORIGINAL DOTS
Gold   GP71GD   ⅞yd (80cm)
ASIAN CIRCLES
Orange   GP89OR   ⅜yd (35cm)
RADIATION
Red   GP115RD   ¾yd (70cm)
SHOT COTTON
Clementine   SC80   ¼yd (25cm)
WOVEN NARROW STRIPE
Red   WNS RD   ¼yd (25cm)

Appliqué Fabrics
For some fabrics only a tiny amount is needed, so you could use scraps from other Rowan projects.
TENTS
Slate   BM03SE   ¼yd (25cm)
SHIRT STRIPES
Brown   GP51BR   ⅜yd (35cm)
GUINEA FLOWER
Apricot   GP59AP   ¼yd (25cm)
ABORIGINAL DOTS
Periwinkle   GP71PE   ¼yd (25cm)
MILLEFIORE
Red   GP92RD   ⅛yd (15cm)
SHOT COTTON
Persimmon   SC07   ⅛yd (15cm)
Scarlet   SC44   ⅛yd (15cm)
Lipstick   SC82   scraps
Blueberry   SC88   ⅛yd (15cm)
WOVEN CATERPILLAR STRIPE
Dusk   WCS DU   ⅛yd (15cm)

Backing Fabric 3¼yd (3m)
We suggest these fabrics for backing
RADIATION Brown, GP115BR
RINGS Beige, BM15BE
ASIAN CIRCLES Orange, GP89OR

Binding
STRAWS
Pink   BM08PK ½yd (45cm)

Batting
54in x 60in (137cm x 152.5cm)

Quilting thread
Toning machine quilting thread
Toning perlé embroidery threads

101

CUTTING OUT

Rectangle 1 Cut 7¾in x 20¾in (19.75cm x 52.75cm) in GP71GD

Rectangle 2 Cut 7¾in x 6in (19.75cm x 15.25cm) in BM15BE

Rectangle 3 Cut 7¾in x 7½in (19.75cm x 19cm) in GP89OR

Rectangle 4 Cut 7¾in x 8½in (19.75cm x 21.5cm) in SC80

Rectangle 5 Cut 12in x 8¾in (30.5cm x 22.25cm) in BM15BE

Rectangle 6 Cut 12in x 8¼in (30.5cm x 21cm) in GP89OR

Rectangle 7 Cut 12in x 8¼in (30.5cm x 21cm) in GP59BR

Rectangle 8 Cut 12in x 11in (30.5cm x 28cm) in GP20PP

Rectangle 9 Cut 12in x 7in (30.5cm x 17.75cm) in WNS RD

Rectangle 10 Cut 16½in x 10¼in (42cm x 26cm) in GP20PP

Rectangle 11 Cut 16½in x 5in (42cm x 12.75cm) in WNS RD

Rectangle 12 Cut 12½in x 27in (31.75cm x 68.5cm) in GP71GD

Rectangle 13 Cut 4½in x 27in (11.5cm x 68.5cm) in SC80

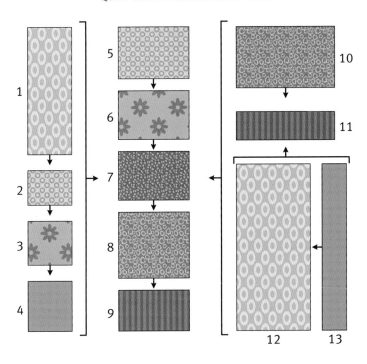

Border Cut 4 strips 6in (15.25cm) across the width of the fabric in GP115RD, join as necessary and cut 2 borders 41¼in x 6in (104.75cm x 15.25cm) for the quilt sides and 2 strips 35¼in x 6in (89.5cm x 15.25cm) for the quilt top and bottom. Also cut 4 corner posts 6in (15.25cm) square in GP59BR.

Appliqué Shapes
Large Circle Cut 1 in GP71PE, SC44 and fussy cut 1 in GP59AP centring on a bloom.
Medium Circle Cut 4 in GP71PE, 3 in SC07, 2 in GP92RD, 1 in SC44, SC88 and fussy cut 1 in GP59AP centring on a bloom.
Small Circle Cut 2 in SC88 and 1 in SC07.
Flower Centres Cut 4 in SC88, 3 in GP71PE, 2 in SC44, SC82 and 1 in SC80 using the flower centre template. Also fussy cut 4 blooms from GP59AP.
Leaf Cut 8 in WCS DU and 3 in GP51BR.
Vases Using the vase template cut 2 in BM03SE and cut a rectangle 7½in x 5¾in (19cm x 14.75cm) in WNS RD, note the stripe direction is vertical.
Flower Stems Cut varying lengths and widths of the fabric ranging from 4in to12½in (10cm to 31.75cm) in length and 7/8in to 1¼in (2.25cm to 3.25cm) in width. Also refer to the photograph. Cut 17 in GP51BR and 1 in WCS DU.
Binding Cut 5 strips 2½in (6.5cm) across the width of the fabric in BM08PK.

Backing Cut 2 pieces 30½in x 54in (77.5cm x 137cm) in backing fabric.

MAKING THE QUILT CENTRE
Use a ¼in (6mm) seam allowance throughout. Referring to the quilt centre assembly diagram for fabric placement, piece 3 columns as shown in the quilt centre assembly diagram. Join the columns to form the quilt centre.

APPLIQUÉ AND BORDER
Refer to the Patchwork Know How Hand Appliqué section on page 139 for appliqué techniques and to the quilt assembly diagram and photographs for appliqué positioning and fabrics. Press a ¼in (6mm) seam allowance rounds each vase shape. Apply the vases to the quilt centre, leaving the top unstitched for now. Again using a ¼in (6mm) seam

Pauline says:
When doing hand appliqué Pauline recommends dampening the fabric and finger pressing the seam allowances of the leaves and stems before pinning the shapes and stitching into place.

allowance, apply the leaves and flower stems finger pressing as you go. Tuck the stems into the vases as appropriate. Finish the bottoms of all other stems neatly (the tops will be covered by flowers). Stitch down the top edges of the vases. Make the flowers using the card template method. Apply the centres to the flowers before adding to the quilt centre. Arrange the flowers and stitch into place. Add the border as shown in the quilt assembly diagram.

FINISHING THE QUILT

Press the quilt top. Seam the backing pieces using a ¼in (6mm) seam allowance to form a piece approx. 54in x 60in (137cm x 152.5cm). Layer the quilt top, batting and backing and baste together (see page 140). Using toning machine quilting thread quilt in the ditch around the rectangle background shapes, then using toning perlé embroidery threads hand quilt the striped background rectangles following the fabric stripes about 1½in (3.75cm) apart. Hand quilt around the flowers and flower centres again with perlé embroidery threads. Trim the quilt edges and attach the binding (see page 141).

QUILT ASSEMBLY DIAGRAM

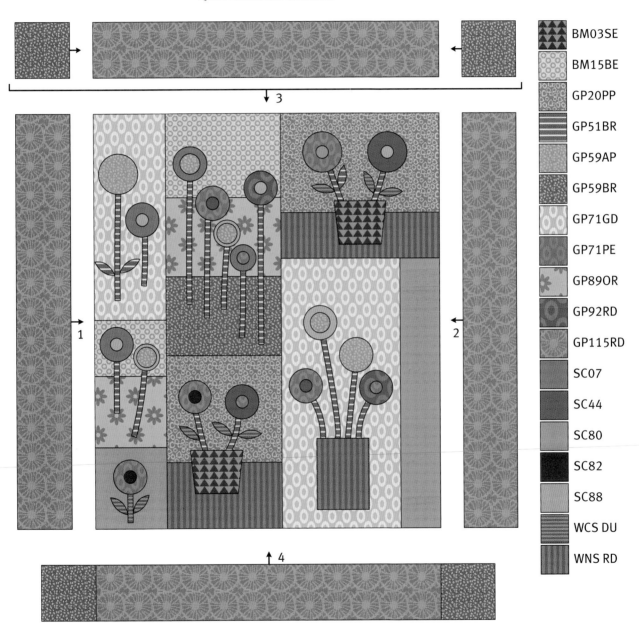

BM03SE	
BM15BE	
GP20PP	
GP51BR	
GP59AP	
GP59BR	
GP71GD	
GP71PE	
GP89OR	
GP92RD	
GP115RD	
SC07	
SC44	
SC80	
SC82	
SC88	
WCS DU	
WNS RD	

driftwood my fair lady **

Brandon Mably

The blocks for this quilt are made by piecing 2 narrow and 1 wide fabric strip into 'strip sets' which are then cut into equilateral triangles (Template PP). The triangles are then pieced into hexagonal blocks, each strip set yields 2 different blocks, (see block assembly diagram c). The blocks are joined into rows along with additional background triangles cut using template PP. A second triangle shape (Template QQ & Reverse QQ) is used to complete the quilt top and bottom.

SIZE OF QUILT
The finished quilt will measure approx. 71in x 81½in (180cm x 207cm).

MATERIALS
Patchwork Fabrics
WAVES
Desert	BM04DS	¼yd (25cm)

STRAWS
Grey	BM08GY	½yd (45cm)

BABBLE
Ochre	BM13OC	⅜yd (35cm)
White	BM13WH	⅜yd (35cm)

RINGS
Beige	BM15BE	⅜yd (35cm)

CLOVER DOTS
Blue	BM23BL	¼yd (25cm)
Pastel	BM23PT	½yd (45cm)

PETRA
Blue	BM24BL	⅝yd (60cm)
Brown	BM24BR	⅜yd (35cm)

MACARONI
Pink	BM25PK	½yd (45cm)

PLAID
Grey	BM26GY	⅜yd (35cm)

SHINGLES
Grey	BM27GY	2½yd (2.3m)

PLINK
Sand	GP109SA	⅝yd (60cm)

BEGONIA COLUMNS
Grey	PJ44GY	⅜yd (35cm)

LACY
Grey	PJ46GY	½yd (45cm)

Backing Fabric 5⅜yd (4.9m)
We suggest these fabrics for backing
ROPE Neutral, BM28NE
CLOVER DOTS Pastel, BM23PT
LACY Grey, PJ46GY

Binding
WRINKLE
Blue	BM18BL	⅝yd (60cm)

Batting
79in x 90in (201cm x 228.5cm).

Quilting thread
Toning machine quilting thread and hand quilting thread.

Templates

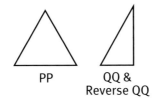

PP   QQ &
        Reverse QQ

CUTTING OUT
Importation information. Please read carefully before cutting any fabrics. Usually we recommend removing the selvedges before using fabrics, but in this case the fabrics for strip sets need to be as wide as possible, so leave the selvedges in place.

Template PP Background fabric BM27GY only. Cut 5¾in (14.75cm) wide strips across the width of the fabric. Each strip will give you 11 patches per full width. Cut 102.

Template QQ and Reverse QQ
Background fabric BM27GY only. Cut 3½in (9cm) wide strips across the width of the fabric. Each strip will give you 12 patches per 45in (114cm) wide fabric. Cut 14, then reverse the template by turning it over and cut a further 14. Total 28 Triangles.

Borders Cut 8 strips 1in (2.5cm) across the width of the fabric, join as necessary and cut 2 strips 1in x 82in (2.5cm x 208.25cm) for the quilt sides and 2 strips 1in x 72½in (2.5cm x 184cm) for the quilt top and bottom in BM27GY, these borders are generous, trim to fit exactly.

Strip Set Fabric Cut 2¾in (7cm) wide strips across the width of the fabric. Cut 3 in BM24BL, GP109SA, PJ46GY, 2 in BM04DS, BM13WH, BM15BE, BM23BL, BM23PT, BM26GY, PJ44GY and 1 in BM08GY. Total 24 wide strips.
Cut 2in (5cm) wide strips across the width of the fabric. Cut 7 in BM25PK, 5 in BM08GY, BM23PT, BM24BL, GP109SA, 4 in BM13OC, BM24BR, 3 in BM26GY, PJ46GY, 2 in BM13WH, BM15BE, PJ44GY and 1 in BM23BL. Total 48 narrow strips.

Binding Cut 8 strips 2½in (6.5cm) wide x width of fabric in BM18BL.

Backing Cut 2 pieces 40in x 90in (101.5cm x 228.5cm) in backing fabric.

CUTTING DIAGRAM

Start cutting 1in (2.5cm) from the selvedge using template PP

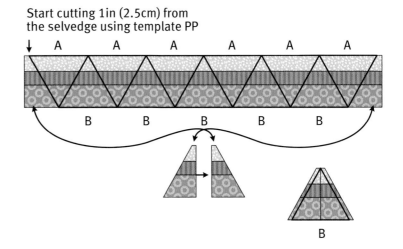

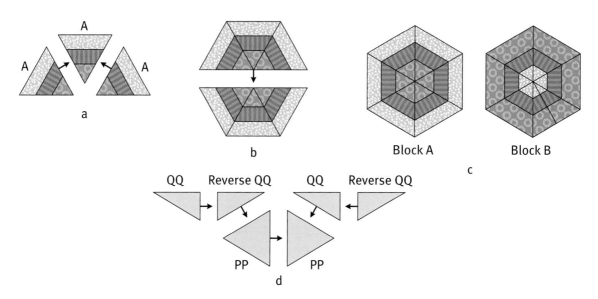

MAKING THE BLOCKS

Use a ¼in (6mm) seam allowance throughout. First sort all the fabric strips into sets. Each set has 1 x 2¾ in (7cm) wide strip and 2 x 2in (5mm) wide strips, there are enough strips for 24 sets. Each strip set will yield 2 blocks, Block A and Block B, which look very different (see block assembly diagram c). There are enough sets to yield 48 blocks, only 46 are used in the quilt, the spare blocks could be used for a matching cushion or pillow. When sorting your fabric strips look for the blocks with the larger centre sections (Block A) to identify the fabric combinations.

Join the first strip set as shown in the cutting diagram, press carefully. Starting 1in (2.5cm) in from the selvedge cut the strip set into equilateral triangles using Template PP. You will get 6 'A' triangles and 5 'B' triangles per set. Take the 2 end pieces of the strip, join as shown and cut a sixth 'B' triangle, centring on the seam. Take the 6 'A' triangles and join to form Block A following diagrams a and b. Next take the 6 'B' triangles and join in the same way to form Block B. Make the strip sets, cut and piece one at a time to prevent the triangles being mixed up. Make a total of 46 blocks (23 Block A and 23 Block B).

MAKING THE QUILT

Lay out the blocks as shown in the quilt assembly diagram filling the gaps with the background triangles. Along the top and bottom edges of the quilt there are 6 pieced background sections. Join template PP and QQ & Reverse QQ background triangles as shown in diagram d for these sections. Carefully separate the diagonal rows and join as shown in the quilt assembly diagram. Join the rows to form the quilt centre. Finally trim the borders to fit and add in the order indicated.

FINISHING THE QUILT

Press the quilt top. Seam the backing pieces using a ¼in (6mm) seam allowance to form a piece approx. 79in x 90in (201cm x 228.5cm). Layer the quilt top, batting and backing and baste together (see page 140). Using a toning machine quilting thread, quilt-in-the-ditch around the hexagons and along the quilt top and bottom, as shown in the quilting diagram. Also, hand quilt around the seams in each block as shown. Trim the quilt edges and attach the binding (see page 141).

QUILTING DIAGRAM

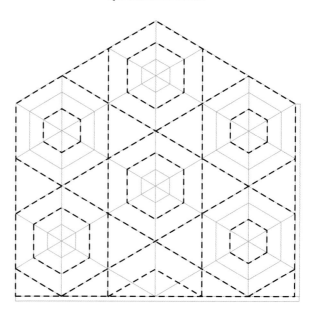

QUILT ASSEMBLY DIAGRAM

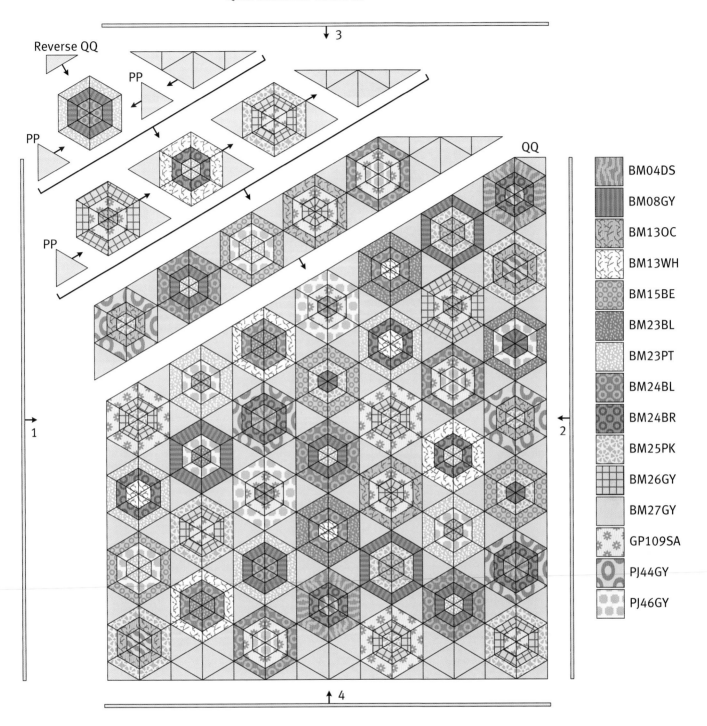

Reverse QQ

PP

PP

PP

QQ

1

2

3

4

BM04DS
BM08GY
BM13OC
BM13WH
BM15BE
BM23BL
BM23PT
BM24BL
BM24BR
BM25PK
BM26GY
BM27GY
GP109SA
PJ44GY
PJ46GY

mardi gras star **

Liza Prior Lucy

The cheerful star blocks in this quilt finish to 12in (30.5cm) square and are made using 3 squares (Templates T, U and V) and 2 two triangles (Templates W and X). The blocks are set in straight rows and are surrounded with a simple border to complete the quilt.

SIZE OF QUILT
The finished quilt will measure approx. 57in x 69in (145cm x 175cm).

MATERIALS
Patchwork and Border Fabrics
BABBLE

Charcoal	BM13CC	⅛yd (15cm)
Red	BM13RD	⅜yd (35cm)
Slate	BM13SE	⅜yd (35cm)

ROMAN GLASS

Byzantine	GP01BY	⅜yd (35cm)
Gold	GP01GD	⅜yd (35cm)
Red	GP01RD	¼yd (25cm)

PAPERWEIGHT

Purple	GP20PU	⅜yd (35cm)

SHIRT STRIPES

Cobalt	GP51CB	⅜yd (35cm)

SPOT

Brown	GP70BR	⅜yd (35cm)
Magenta	GP70MG	⅜yd (35cm)
Purple	GP70PU	⅛yd (15cm)
Red	GP70RD	⅜yd (35cm)
Taupe	GP70TA	⅜yd (35cm)
Turquoise	GP70TQ	⅜yd (35cm)

ABORIGINAL DOTS

Charcoal	GP71CC	⅜yd (35cm)
Ochre	GP71OC	⅜yd (35cm)
Ocean	GP71ON	⅜yd (35cm)
Purple	GP71PU	⅜yd (35cm)
Taupe	GP71TA	¼yd (25cm)
Terracotta	GP71TC	⅛yd (15cm)

MILLEFIORE

Blue	GP92BL	⅜yd (35cm)
Green	GP92GN	⅜yd (35cm)
Tomato	GP92TM	⅜yd (35cm)

RADIATION

Red	GP115RD	¼yd (25cm)

KITE TAILS

Black	GP122BK	¼yd (25cm)
Red	GP122RD	¼yd (25cm)

LACY

Dark	PJ46DK	¼yd (25cm)
Warm	PJ46WM	1⅛yd (1m)

Backing Fabric 3⅞yd (3.6m)
We suggest these fabrics for backing
KITE TAILS Black, GP122BK or Red, GP122RD
MILLEFIORE Tomato, GP92TM

Binding
BABBLE

Slate	BM13SE	⅝yd (60cm)

Batting
65in x 77in (165cm x 195.5cm)

Quilting thread
Toning machine quilting thread

Templates

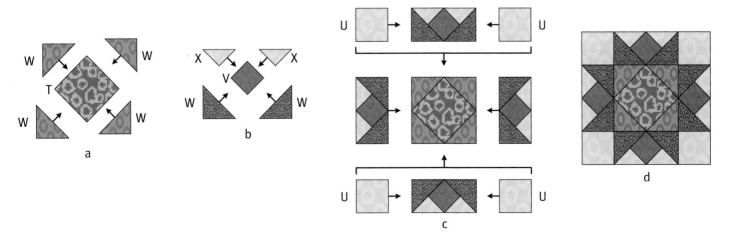

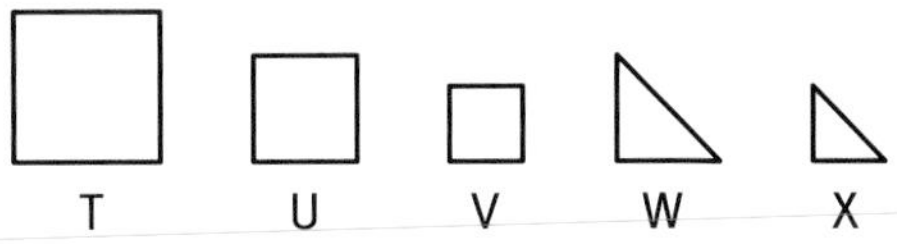

CUTTING OUT
For the best use of the fabric cut the large template shapes first, then trim remaining fabric strips for smaller shapes. We have listed the template shapes in order of cutting size to help with this.

Border Cut 6 strips 5in (12.75cm) across the width of the fabric in PJ46WM. Join strips as necessary and cut 2 strips 60½in x 5in (153.75cm x 12.75cm) for the side borders and 2 strips 57½in x 5in (146cm x 12.75cm) for the top and bottom borders.

Template T Cut 4¾in (12cm) strips across the width of the fabric. Each strip will give you 8 squares per full width. Cut 4 in GP115RD, GP122BK, GP122RD, PJ46DK and PJ46WM. Total 20 squares.

Template X Cut 4¼in (10.75cm) wide strips across the width of the fabric. Each strip will give you 36 triangles per full width. Cut 4¼in (10.75cm) squares, then using the template as a guide cut each square twice diagonally to make 4 triangles. This will ensure the long side of the triangles will not have a bias edge. Cut 8 in BM13RD, BM13SE, GP01BY, GP01GD, GP01RD, GP20PU, GP51CB, GP70BR, GP70MG, GP70RD, GP70TA, GP70TQ, GP71CC, GP71OC, GP71ON, GP71PU, GP71TA, GP92BL, GP92GN and GP92TM. Total 160 triangles.

Template W Cut 3⅞in (9.75cm) wide strips across the width of the fabric. Each strip will give you 20 triangles per full width. Cut 12 in BM13SE, GP01BY, GP01GD, GP20PU, GP70BR, GP70MG, GP70PU, GP70TA, GP70TQ, GP71CC,

BLOCK ASSEMBLY DIAGRAMS

GP71OC, GP71ON, GP71PU, GP92BL, GP92TM, 8 in BM13CC, GP01RD, GP51MD, GP70RD, GP71TA, GP71TC, GP92GN and 4 in BM13RD. Total 240 Triangles.

Template U Cut 3½in (9cm) wide strips across the width of the fabric. Each strip will give you 11 squares per full width. Cut 4 in BM13RD, BM13SE, GP01BY, GP01GD, GP01RD, GP20PU, GP51CB, GP70BR, GP70MG, GP70RD, GP70TA, GP70TQ, GP71CC, GP71OC, GP71ON, GP71PU, GP71TA, GP92BL, GP92GN and GP92TM. Total 80 squares.

Template V Cut 2⅝in (6.75cm) wide strips across the width of the fabric. Each strip will give you 15 squares per full width. Cut 4 in BM13CC, BM13RD, BM13SE, GP01BY, GP01GD, GP20PU, GP51CB, GP70MG, GP70PU, GP70RD, GP70TA, GP70TQ, GP71CC, GP71OC, GP71ON, GP71PU, GP71TC, GP92BL, GP92GN and GP92TM. Total 80 Squares.

Binding Cut 7 strips 2½in (6.5cm) wide across the width of the fabric in BM13SE.

Backing Cut 1 piece 40in x 65in (101.5cm x 165cm) and 1 piece 38in x 65in (96.5cm x 165cm) in backing fabric.

MAKING THE BLOCKS
Use a ¼in (6mm) seam allowance throughout. Piece 20 blocks following block assembly diagrams a, b and c, the completed block is shown in diagram d. Refer to the quilt assembly diagram for fabric placement.

MAKING THE QUILT
Join the blocks together into 5 rows of 4 blocks, join the rows to make the quilt centre. Add the side, then top and bottom borders to the quilt centre as shown in the quilt assembly diagram.

FINISHING THE QUILT
Press the quilt top. Seam the backing pieces using a ¼in (6mm) seam allowance to form a piece approx. 65in x 77in (165cm x 195.5cm). Layer the quilt top, batting and backing and baste together (see page 140). Using mauve machine quilting thread, quilt in a 'twirly' pattern over the quilt centre and borders. Trim the quilt edges and attach the binding (see page 141).

QUILT ASSEMBLY DIAGRAM

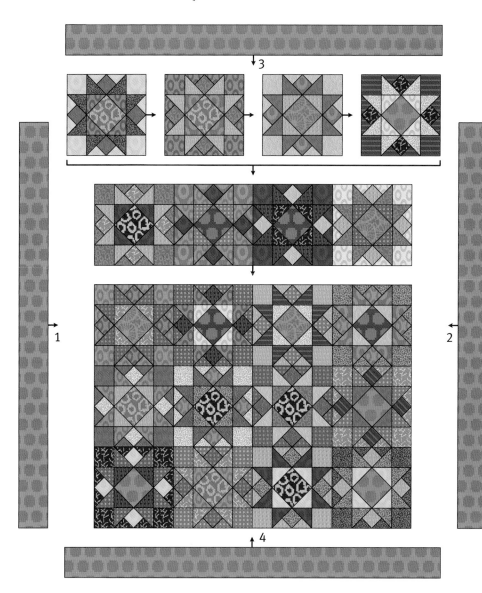

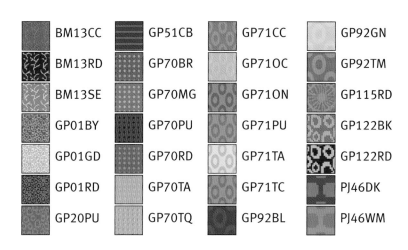

BM13CC	GP51CB	GP71CC	GP92GN
BM13RD	GP70BR	GP71OC	GP92TM
BM13SE	GP70MG	GP71ON	GP115RD
GP01BY	GP70PU	GP71PU	GP122BK
GP01GD	GP70RD	GP71TA	GP122RD
GP01RD	GP70TA	GP71TC	PJ46DK
GP20PU	GP70TQ	GP92BL	PJ46WM

hot matisse villa **

Roberta Horton

The blocks in this quilt are made using 2 square patch shapes (Templates C & E) and 1 triangle patch shape (Template D) and are set 'on point' into rows using 2 triangle patch shapes (Templates F and G). You'll find half template F on page XX. Take a large piece of paper, fold, place the edge of template F to the fold of paper, trace around shape and cut out. Open out for the complete template. The pieced rows are interspaced with sashing strips and then surrounded with a simple inner border. The quilt is then finished with an outer border with corner posts (Template E).

SIZE OF QUILT
The finished quilt will measure approx.
72½ x 73¼in (184cm x 186cm).

MATERIALS
Patchwork Fabrics
AURORA
Green   BM21GN   ⅜yd (35cm)
LOTUS LEAF
Yellow   GP29YE   1⅝yd (1.5m)
SPOT
Green   GP70GN   ⅜yd (35cm)
LINE DANCE
Lavender   GP116LV   ⅝yd (60cm)
VARIEGATED LEAVES
Red   PJ39RD   ½yd (45cm)
JAPANESE CHRYSANTHEMUM
Green   PJ41GN   ¼yd (25cm)
PRIMULA
Magenta   PJ42MG   ½yd (45cm)

Sashing and Border Fabrics
WRINKLE
Black   BM18BK   ½yd (45cm)
RADIATION
Red   GP115RD   1½yd (1.4m)
PRIMULA
Black   PJ42BK   ¾yd (70cm)

Backing Fabric 4¾yd (4.4m)
We suggest these fabrics for backing
AURORA Black BM21BK or Green BM21GN
VARIEGATED LEAVES Red PJ39RD

Binding
DAPPLE
Regal   BM05RE   ⅝yd (60cm)

Batting
80in x 80in (203cm x 203cm)

Quilting thread
Toning machine quilting thread

Templates

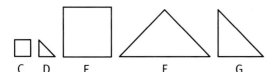

C   D   E   F   G

CUTTING OUT
Template C Cut 2½in (6.5cm) strips across the width of the fabric. Each strip will give you 16 triangles per full width. Cut 20 in GP116LV.
Template D Cut 2⅞in (7.25cm) strips across the width of the fabric. Each strip will give you 26 triangles per full width. Cut 120 in GP116LV, 60 in BM21GN and GP70GN.
Template E Cut 6½in (16.5cm) strips across the width of the fabric. Each strip will give you 6 squares per full width. Cut 10 in PJ39RD and PJ42MG. Also Cut 4 in PJ41GN for outer border corner posts.
Template F Cut 12½in (31.75cm) strips across the width of the fabric in GP29YE. Each strip will give you 12 patches per full width. Cut 8 x 12½in (31.75cm) squares, then using the template as a guide cut each square twice diagonally to make 4 triangles. This will ensure the long side of the triangle will not have a bias edge. Cut 32 in GP29YE.
Template G Cut 6½in (16.5cm) strips across the width of the fabric. Each strip will give you 12 patches per full width. Cut 16 in GP29YE.
Sashing Cut 5 strips 4½in (11.5cm) across the width of the fabric in PJ42BK. Join strips as necessary and cut 3 sashing strips 57in x 4½in (144.75cm x 11.5cm).
Inner Border Cut 6 strips 2½in (6.5cm) across the width of the fabric in BM18BK. Join strips as necessary and cut 2 strips 61¾in x 2½in (157cm x 6.5cm) for the side inner borders and 2 strips 57in x 2½in (144.75cm x 6.5cm) for the top and bottom inner borders.
Outer Border Cut 7 strips 6½in (16.5cm) across the width of the fabric in GP115RD. Join strips as necessary and cut 2 strips 61¾in x 6½in (157cm x 16.5cm) for the side outer borders and 2 strips 61in x 6½in (155cm x 16.5cm) for the top and bottom outer borders.

Binding Cut 8 strips 2½in (6.5cm) across width of the fabric in BM05RE.

Backing Cut 2 pieces 40in x 80in (101.5cm x 203cm) in backing fabric.

MAKING THE BLOCKS AND ROWS
Use a ¼in (6mm) seam allowance throughout. Piece 20 blocks following block assembly diagrams a and b, the finished block can be seen in diagram c. There are 2 colourways for the blocks, make 10 of each referring to the quilt assembly diagram for fabric placement. Piece the blocks together into 4 rows of 5 blocks using the Template F and G triangles to set the blocks 'on point' as shown in the row assembly diagram.

MAKING THE QUILT
Interspace the pieced rows with sashing strips as shown in the quilt assembly diagram. Join the top and bottom, then side inner borders to the quilt centre. Join the side outer borders to the quilt centre, join a corner post to each end of the top and bottom outer borders and join to the quilt centre.

BLOCK ASSEMBLY DIAGRAMS

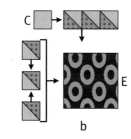

a

b

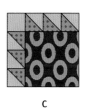

c

ROW ASSEMBLY DIAGRAM

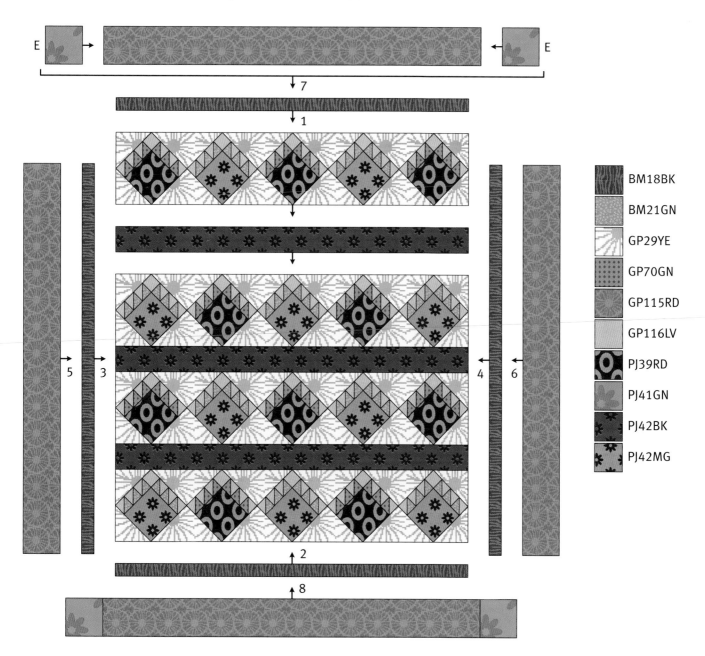

FINISHING THE QUILT
Press the quilt top. Seam the backing
pieces using a ¼in (6mm) seam
allowance to form a piece approx. 80in
x 80in (203cm x 203cm). Layer the quilt
top, batting and backing and baste
together (see page 140). Using toning
machine quilting thread, quilt in the ditch
around the blocks, Free motion meander
quilt following fabric designs in the large
triangles, squares and borders. Trim the
quilt edges and attach the binding (see
page 141).

QUILT ASSEMBLY DIAGRAM

BM18BK
BM21GN
GP29YE
GP70GN
GP115RD
GP116LV
PJ39RD
PJ41GN
PJ42BK
PJ42MG

twilight two up two down **

Brandon Mably

Brandon's traditional schoolhouse blocks are made using a square patch (Template R), a lozenge patch (Template Q), a rectangle patch (Template S) and a triangle patch (Template D). The doors and windows are appliquéd using adhesive web, we suggest using the non−sew type as the shapes are quite small, however instructions for both sew and non−sew adhesive web can be found in the Patchwork Know How section in the back of the book. The blocks are interspaced with sashing and framed with a simple border to complete the quilt.

SIZE OF QUILT
The finished quilt will measure approx.
44in x 50in (112cm x 127cm).

MATERIALS
Patchwork and Sashing Fabrics
DAPPLE

Green	BM05GN	¼yd (25cm)
Regal	BM05RE	¾yd (70cm)

STRAWS

Midnight	BM08MD	⅜yd (35cm)

RINGS

Blue	BM15BL	⅜yd (35cm)

WRINKLE

Black	BM18BK	¼yd (25cm)

HERRINGBONE STRIPE

Blue	BM19BL	¼yd (25cm)

BEADED TENTS

Dark	BM20DK	⅜yd (35cm)

MACARONI

Cool	BM25CL	⅜yd (35cm)

PLAID

Blue	BM26BL	⅜yd (35cm)
Green	BM26GN	⅛yd (15cm)

SHIRT STRIPES

Cobalt	GP51CB	⅛yd (15cm)
Red	GP51RD	⅛yd (15cm)

SPOT

Brown	GP70BR	¼yd (25cm)
Purple	GP70PU	¼yd (25cm)

MILLEFIORE

Blue	GP92BL	¼yd (25cm)

Appliqué Fabrics
BABBLE

Red	BM13RD	⅛yd (15cm)

MACARONI

Spice	BM25SI	⅛yd (15cm)

SPOT

Tobacco	GP70TO	⅛yd (15cm)

Border Fabric
DANCING PAISLEY

Purple	BM22PU	½yd (45cm)

Backing Fabric 3⅛yd (2.9m)
We suggest these fabrics for backing
MACARONI Cool, BM25CL
PLAID Blue, BM26BL or Green, BM26GN

Binding
HERRINGBONE STRIPE

Black	BM19BK	½yd (45cm)

Batting
52in x 58in (132cm x 147.5cm).

Quilting Thread
Toning machine quilting thread.

You Will Also Need
Non−sew adhesive web for appliqué.

Templates

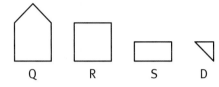

This quilt also uses the appliqué shapes on page 137.

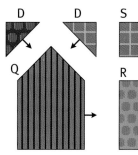
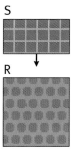
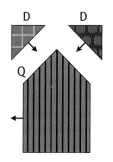
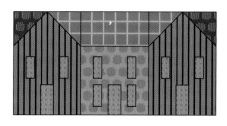

a

b

CUTTING OUT

Cut the fabric in the order stated to prevent waste. Use leftover strips for subsequent templates trimming as necessary.

Sashing Cut 7 strips 2½in (6.25cm) across the width of the fabric in BM05RE. Cut 5 horizontal sashing strips 2½in x 40½in (6.25cm x 102.75cm) and 12 short sashing strips 2½in x 6½in (6.25cm x 16.5cm).

Template Q Cut 4½in (11.5cm) strips across the width of the fabric. Each strip will give you 6 patches per full width. Cut 6 in BM06MD, BM19BL, BM20DK, BM25CL, 4 in BM15BL, BM18BK and BM26BL. Total 36 patches.

Template R Cut 4½in (11.5cm) strips across the width of the fabric. Cut 4 in BM26BL, 3 in GP70BR, 2 in BM05GN, BM18BK, GP70PU, 1 in BM08MD, BM15BL, BM20DK, BM25CL and GP92BL. Total 18 squares.

Template D Cut 2⅞in (7.25cm) strips across the width of the fabric. Each strip will give you 26 patches per full width. Cut 36 in BM05RE, 8 in GP51RD, 6 in BM26GN, GP51CB, GP92BL, 4 in GP70PU, 2 in BM15BL, BM25CL and BM26BL. Total 72 triangles.

Template S Cut 2½in (6.25cm) strips across the width of the fabric. Cut 4 in GP51RD, 3 in BM26GN, GP51CB, GP92BL, 2 in GP70PU, 1 in BM15BL, BM25CL and BM26BL. Total 18 rectangles.

Borders Cut 5 strips 2½in (6.25cm) across the width of the fabric in BM22PU. Join as necessary and cut 2 borders 2½in x 50½in (6.25cm x 128.25cm) for the quilt sides and 2 borders 2½in x 40½in (6.25cm x 102.75cm) for the quilt top and bottom.

Appliqué Shapes Trace 54 doors and 144 windows onto the paper side of your adhesive web leaving a ¼in (6mm) gap between the shapes. Roughly cut out the shapes about ⅛in (3mm) outside your drawn line. Bond the shapes to the REVERSE of the fabrics. Bond 21 doors in GP70TO, 18 in BM25SI and 15 in BM13RD. Bond 56 windows in GP70TO, 48 in BM25SI and 40 in BM13RD.

Binding Cut 5 strips 2½in (6.5cm) wide across the width of the fabric in BM19BK.

Backing Cut 1 piece 40in x 52in (101.5cm x 132cm) and 1 piece 19in x 52in (48.25cm x 132cm) in backing fabric.

MAKING THE BLOCKS

Use a ¼in (6mm) seam allowance throughout. Use the quilt assembly diagram as a guide to fabric placement. Piece 18 schoolhouse blocks, as shown in block assembly diagram a. The finished block can be seen in diagram b. This also shows the positions of the appliqué doors and windows. Full instructions for using adhesive web for appliqué can be found in the Patchwork Know How section on page 139.

Remove the backing paper from the appliqué shapes and position carefully as shown in diagram b. The doors should be aligned with the raw edge of the block, so that the bottom ¼in (6mm) will be stitched into the seam when the block is joined to the sashing later. Bond the shapes into place according to the manufacturer's instructions.

MAKING THE QUILT

Arrange the blocks into 6 rows of 3 blocks as shown in the quilt assembly diagram, interspacing the blocks with the short sashing strips. Join the blocks into rows, then interspace the rows with the horizontal sashing strips and join. Finally add top and bottom, then the side borders to complete the quilt.

FINISHING THE QUILT

Press the quilt top. Seam the backing pieces using a ¼in (6mm) seam allowance to form a piece approx. 52in x 58in (132cm x 147.5cm). Layer the quilt top, batting and backing and baste together (see page 140). Using toning machine quilting thread, stitch in the ditch in all the seams, and quilt ⅛in (3mm) in from the edge of all the appliqué shapes. In the sashing and borders free motion quilt following the designs in the fabrics. Trim the quilt edges and attach the binding (see page 141).

QUILT ASSEMBLY DIAGRAM

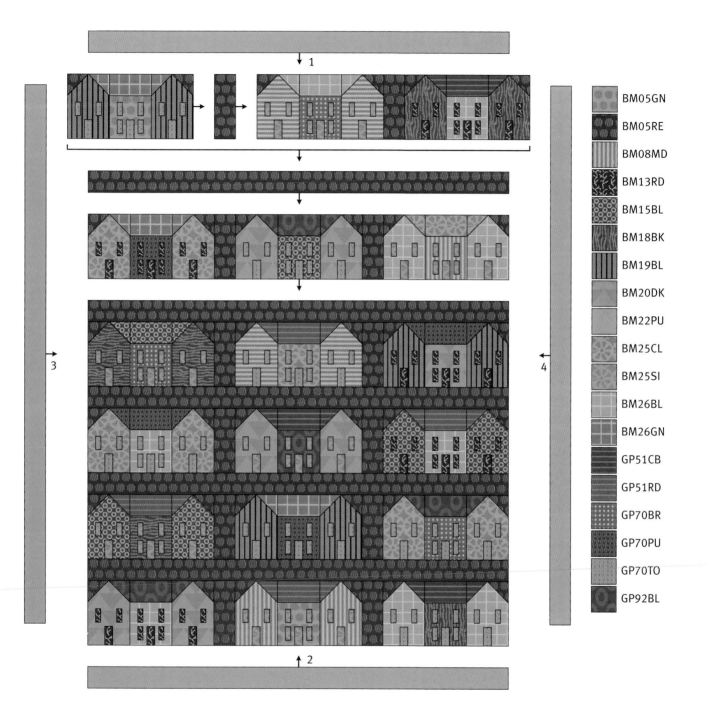

BM05GN
BM05RE
BM08MD
BM13RD
BM15BL
BM18BK
BM19BL
BM20DK
BM22PU
BM25CL
BM25SI
BM26BL
BM26GN
GP51CB
GP51RD
GP70BR
GP70PU
GP70TO
GP92BL

dusky african huts *

Pauline Smith

This striking picture quilt is surprisingly easy to make as none of the patch shapes are tiny or fiddly, a good one for a beginner. Each block is based around a large rectangle (Template K) used for the main hut wall. The roof of the hut is made with a small triangle (Template H) and a large triangle (Template J) and the background is made using 3 rectangle patch shapes (Templates L, M and N). The blocks are set in simple rows to complete the quilt.

SIZE OF QUILT
The finished quilt will measure approx. 40in x 40in (102cm x 102cm).

MATERIALS
Patchwork Fabrics
TENTS

Slate	BM03SE	¼yd (25cm)

HERRINGBONE STRIPE

Red	BM19RD	¼yd (25cm)

PAPERWEIGHT

Paprika	GP20PP	¼yd (25cm)

ABORIGINAL DOTS

Periwinkle	GP71PE	⅜yd (35cm)

SHOT COTTON

Clementine	SC80	⅛yd (15cm)
True Cobalt	SC45	⅛yd (15cm)
Aegean	SC46	¼yd (25cm)
Magenta	SC81	⅛yd (15cm)
Lipstick	SC82	⅛yd (15cm)
Blueberry	SC88	⅜yd (35cm)

WOVEN ALTERNATING STRIPE

Yellow	WAS YE	¼yd (25cm)

WOVEN BROAD STRIPE

Dark	WBS DK	¼yd (25cm)

WOVEN CATERPILLAR STRIPE

Earth	WCS ER	¼yd (25cm)

WOVEN EXOTIC STRIPE

Purple	WES PU	¼yd (25cm)

WOVEN NARROW STRIPE

Red	WNS RD	¼yd (25cm)

Backing Fabric 2yd (1.8m)
We suggest these fabrics for backing
RINGS Blue BM15BL
ABORIGINAL DOTS Periwinkle GP71PE
WOVEN CATERPILLAR STRIPE Earth, WCS ER

Binding
RINGS

Blue	BM15BL	½yd (45cm)

Batting
48in x 48in (122cm x 122cm).

Quilting thread
Toning machine quilting thread.

Templates

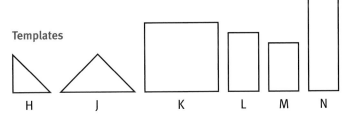

H   J   K   L   M   N

CUTTING OUT
Please cut the patch shapes in the order specified. Reserve leftover fabric strips for following templates and trim as necessary.

Template H Cut 3⅝in (9.25cm) strips across the width of the fabric. Each strip will give you 22 patches per full width. Cut 6 in GP20PP, 4 in BM03SE, SC46, SC82, SC88, WAS YE, 2 in BM19RD, GP71PE and SC81. Total 32 triangles.

Template J Cut 3⅜in (8.5cm) strips across the width of the fabric. Align the template with the long side along the cut edge of the strip, this will ensure the long side of the triangles will not have a bias edge. Each strip will give you 10 patches per full width. Cut 6 in SC45, 4 in SC80, SC81 and 2 in SC46. Total 16 triangles.

Template K Cut 5½in (14cm) strips across the width of the fabric. Each strip will give you 6 patches per full width. Cut 4 in WBS DK, WCS ER, WES PU and WNS RD. Total 16 rectangles.

Template N Cut 2¾in (7cm) strips across the width of the fabric. Each strip will give you 3 patches per full width. Cut 4 in GP71PE, 3 in SC88, 2 in BM03SE, BM19RD, GP20PP, WAS YE and 1 in SC46. Total 16 rectangles.

Template L Cut 2¾in (7cm) strips across the width of the fabric. Each strip will give you 8 patches per full width. Cut 6 in GP20PP, 4 in BM03SE, SC46, SC82, SC88, WAS YE, 2 in BM19RD, GP71PE and SC81. Total 32 rectangles.

Template M Cut 2¾in (7cm) strips across the width of the fabric. Each strip will give you 10 patches per full width. Cut 8 in GP71PE, 6 in SC88, 4 in BM03SE, BM19RD, GP20PP, WAS YE and 2 in SC46. Total 32 rectangles.

BLOCK ASSEMBLY DIAGRAMS

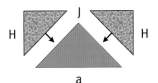

a

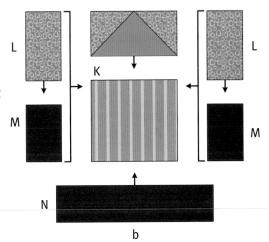

b

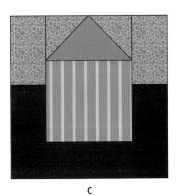

c

Binding Cut 5 strips 2½in (6.5cm) across the width of fabric in BM15BL.

Backing Cut 1 piece 40in x 48in (101.5cm x 122cm), 1 piece 40in x 9in (101.5cm x 23cm) and 1 piece 9in x 9in (23cm x 23cm) in backing fabric.

MAKING THE QUILT

Use a ¼in (6mm) seam allowance throughout and refer to the quilt assembly diagram for fabric combinations. First make the roof sections as shown in diagram a, then assemble the rest of the block as shown in diagram b, the finished block can be seen in diagram c.

Make a total of 16 blocks. Join the blocks into 4 rows of 4 blocks then join the rows to complete the quilt.

FINISHING THE QUILT

Press the quilt top. Seam the backing pieces using a ¼in (6mm) seam allowance to form a piece approx. 48in x 48in (122cm x 122cm). Layer the quilt top, batting and backing and baste together (see page 140). Using a toning machine quilting thread quilt-in-the-ditch around all the blocks, then as shown in the quilting diagram. Trim the quilt edges and attach the binding (see page 141).

QUILTING DIAGRAM

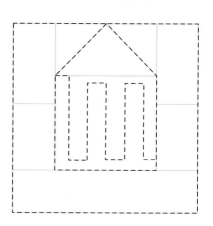

QUILT ASSEMBLY DIAGRAM

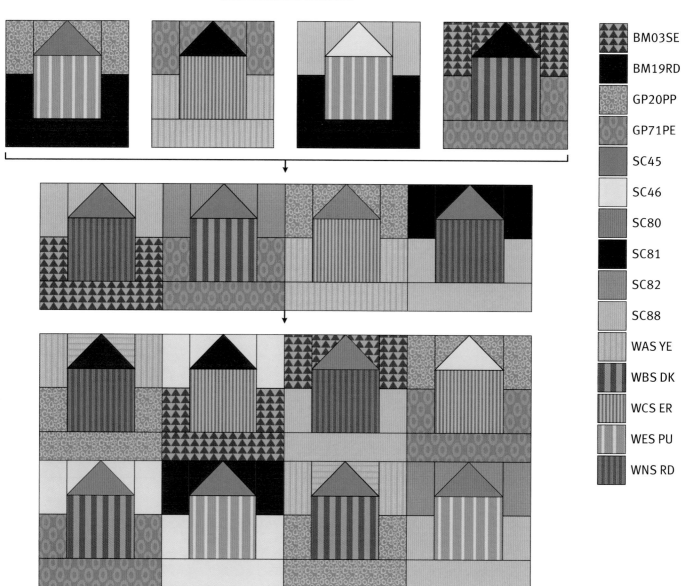

BM03SE
BM19RD
GP20PP
GP71PE
SC45
SC46
SC80
SC81
SC82
SC88
WAS YE
WBS DK
WCS ER
WES PU
WNS RD

grey gridlock *

Liza Prior Lucy

Two blocks, which finish to 12in (30.5cm) square, are alternated to make the centre of this quilt. Block 1 is pieced using a large square (Template R) and a rectangle (cut to size). Block 2 is a 6 x 6 checkerboard pieced using a small square (Template C). The quilt centre is framed with a pieced border again using the large square (Template R).

Templates

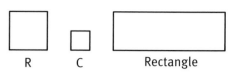

R   C   Rectangle

SIZE OF QUILT
The finished quilt will measure approx. 68in x 80in (172.5cm x 203cm).

MATERIALS
Patchwork Fabrics
BABBLE

Mist	BM13MI	⅜yd (35cm)
White	BM13WH	⅛yd (15cm)

SHINGLES

Grey	BM27GY	⅛yd (15cm)

PAPERWEIGHT

Sludge	GP20SL	¼yd (25cm)

SHIRT STRIPES

Midnight chalk	GP51MC	⅜yd (35cm)

GUINEA FLOWER

Turquoise	GP59TQ	⅜yd (35cm)

SPOT

Apple	GP70AL	¼yd (25cm)
Charcoal	GP70CC	¼yd (25cm)
Chalk	GP70CH	¼yd (25cm)
China Blue	GP70CI	⅜yd (35cm)
Duck Egg	GP70DE	¼yd (25cm)
Grape	GP70GP	⅜yd (35cm)
Lavender	GP70LV	¼yd (25cm)
Soft Blue	GP70SF	⅜yd (35cm)
Teal	GP70TE	¼yd (25cm)

ABORIGINAL DOTS

Taupe	GP71TA	¼yd (25cm)

ASIAN CIRCLES

Chartreuse	GP89CT	⅛yd (15cm)
Turquoise	GP89TQ	⅜yd (35cm)

BIG BLOOMS

Green	GP91GN	½yd (45cm)

MILLEFIORE

Lilac	GP92LI	¼yd (25cm)

RADIATION

Lavender	GP115LV	½yd (45cm)

LINE DANCE

White	GP116WH	¼yd (25cm)

MAP

Pastel	GP120PT	⅜yd (35cm)

GLORY ROSE

Grey	PJ21GY	½yd (45cm)

IRIS AND PEONY

Green	PJ43GN	½yd (45cm)

MIAMI

Pastel	PJ47PT	½yd (45cm)

SHOT COTTON

Ecru	SC24	¼yd (25cm)
Aqua	SC77	⅛yd (15cm)
Ice	SC85	¼yd (25cm)
Galvanised	SC87	⅛yd (15cm)

Backing Fabric 5¼yd (4.8m)
We suggest these fabrics for backing
SHIRT STRIPES Midnight Chalk, GP51MC
MILLEFIORE Lilac, GP92LI
MIAMI Pastel, PJ47PT

Binding Fabric
SHIRT STRIPES
Midnight Chalk GP51MC   ⅝yd (60cm)

Batting
76in x 88in (193cm x 223.5cm)

Quilting thread
Toning machine quilting thread.

CUTTING OUT
Rectangle Cut 4½in (11.5cm) strips across the width of the fabric. Each strip will give you 3 rectangles per full width. Cut 4½in x 12½in (11.5cm x 31.75cm) rectangles, cut 6 in GP91GN, GP115LV, PJ21GY, PJ43GN and PJ47PT. Total 30 Rectangles.

Template R Cut 4½in (11.5cm) strips across the width of the fabric. Each strip will give you 8 squares per full width. Cut 11 in GP70CI, 8 in BM13MI, GP70AL, GP70GP, GP89TQ, GP120PT, 7 in GP70DE, GP70LV, 6 in GP51MC, GP91GN, GP115LV, PJ21GY, PJ43GN, PJ47PT, 5 in GP59TQ, GP70SF, 2 in GP70CC and GP70TE. Total 115 Squares. Reserve leftover strips and trim for template C as necessary.

Template C Cut 2½in (6.5cm) strips across the width of the fabric. Each strip will give you 16 squares per full width. Cut 39 in GP70CH, GP71TA, 33 in GP116WH, 30 in GP51MC, GP70SF, GP92LI, 27 in BM13MI, GP120PT, 24 in GP20SL, GP59TQ, GP70GP, SC85, 21 in GP70CI, GP89TQ, SC24, 15 in BM27GY, GP70CC, GP70DE, GP89CT, SC87, 12 in BM13WH, GP70AL, GP70LV, 9 in GP70TE and 6 in SC77. Total 540 Squares.

Binding Cut 8 strips 2½in (6.5cm) across the width of fabric in GP51MC.

Backing Cut 1 piece 40in x 88in (101.5cm x 223.5cm) and 1 piece 37in x 88in (94cm x 223.5cm) in backing fabric.

BLOCK ASSEMBLY DIAGRAMS

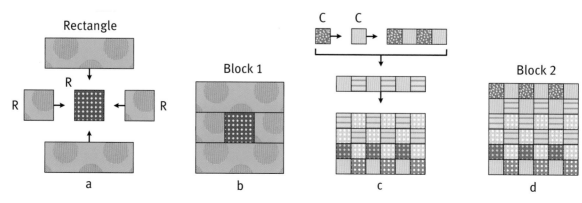

Rectangle

R   R

R   R

a

Block 1

b

C   C

c

Block 2

d

Liza says:

The quilt has been drawn and specified exactly as my sample was made, but it is meant to be a scrappy style quilt, so I suggest substituting scraps and leftovers from other Rowan projects if they fit the colour mood.

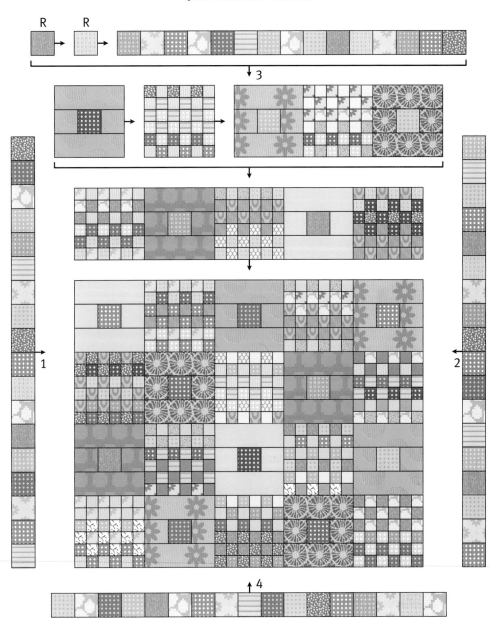

MAKING THE BLOCKS

Use ¼in (6mm) seam allowance throughout. Refer to the quilt assembly diagram for fabric placement.
For Block 1 assemble 3 template R squares with 2 rectangles as shown in Block assembly diagram a. A finished Block 1 is shown in diagram b. Make 15 blocks.
For Block 2, arrange 36 squares into 6 rows of 6 squares as shown in block assembly diagram c. Use the same 2 colours in each horizontal row. Join the rows to form the block. A finished Block 2 is shown in diagram d. Make 15 blocks.

MAKING THE QUILT

Lay out the blocks alternately into 6 rows of 5 blocks, Join the blocks into rows, join the rows to make the quilt centre.

ADDING THE BORDERS

Piece the borders as shown in the quilt assembly diagram and join to the quilt centre in the order indicted.

FINISHING THE QUILT

Press the quilt top. Seam the backing pieces using a ¼in (6mm) seam allowance to form a piece approx. 76in x 88in (193cm x 223.5cm). Layer the quilt top, batting and backing and baste together (see page 140). Using toning machine quilting thread free motion quilt in a meandering pattern. Liza included freestyle floral patterns following the designs in the fabrics on her quilt. Trim the quilt edges and attach the binding (see page 141).

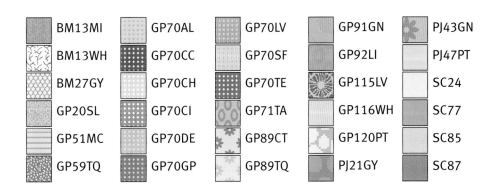

BM13MI	GP70AL	GP70LV	GP91GN	PJ43GN
BM13WH	GP70CC	GP70SF	GP92LI	PJ47PT
BM27GY	GP70CH	GP70TE	GP115LV	SC24
GP20SL	GP70CI	GP71TA	GP116WH	SC77
GP51MC	GP70DE	GP89CT	GP120PT	SC85
GP59TQ	GP70GP	GP89TQ	PJ21GY	SC87

return to rosy *

Liza Prior Lucy

This quilt is suitable for beginners as it is very simple to make. It is the colour and pattern that make it appear complex. Traditional nine–patch blocks are pieced using 1 small square (Template U), these are alternated with large squares, cut to size, and joined into straight set rows. The rows are joined to form the quilt centre. The inner border is pieced from 1 medium square (Template EE), and the outer border is pieced, again using the small square (Template U).

SIZE OF QUILT
The finished quilt will measure approx. 60in x 78in (152.5cm x 198cm).

MATERIALS
Patchwork and Border Fabrics

TENTS		
Driftwood	BM03DR	⅛yd (15cm)
STRAWS		
Orange	BM08OR	⅛yd (15cm)
Red	BM08RD	⅛yd (15cm)
BABBLE		
Charcoal	BM13CC	⅛yd (15cm)
RINGS		
Beige	BM15BE	⅛yd (15cm)
HERRINGBONE STRIPE		
Orange	BM19OR	¼yd (25cm)
MACARONI		
Mustard	BM25MU	¼yd (25cm)
Spice	BM25SI	⅛yd (15cm)
ROMAN GLASS		
Byzantine	GP01BY	¼yd (25cm)
Gold	GP01GD	⅛yd (15cm)
PAPERWEIGHT		
Paprika	GP20PP	⅛yd (15cm)
GUINEA FLOWER		
Green	GP59GN	¼yd (25cm)
ABORIGINAL DOTS		
Forest	GP71FO	⅛yd (15cm)
Ochre	GP71OC	¼yd (25cm)
Purple	GP71PU	¼yd (25cm)
BIG BLOOMS		
Brown	GP91BR	⅜yd (35cm)
MILLEFIORE		
Brown	GP92BR	¼yd (35cm)
Tomato	GP92TM	⅛yd (15cm)
RADIATION		
Brown	GP115BR	⅜yd (35cm)
FOLK ART		
Rust	GP119RU	¼yd (25cm)
MAP		
Brown	GP120BR	⅜yd (35cm)
KITE TAILS		
Mauve	GP122MV	⅜yd (35cm)
POM POM DAHLIAS		
Brown	PJ38BR	⅜yd (35cm)
LACY		
Brown	PJ46BR	⅜yd (35cm)
WOVEN BROAD STRIPE		
Sunset	WBS SS	1¼yd (1.15m)

Backing Fabric 5⅛yd (4.7m)
We suggest these fabrics for backing
KITE TAILS Mauve, GP122MV
RADIATION Brown, GP115BR
POM POM DAHLIAS Brown, PJ38BR

Binding
ABORIGINAL DOTS
Terracotta   GP71TC   ⅝yd (60cm)

Batting
68in x 86in (173cm x 218.5cm)

Quilting thread
Taupe machine quilting thread

Templates

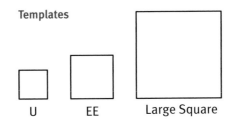

U   EE   Large Square

CUTTING OUT
Cut the shapes in the order specified, always keeping remaining fabric in the largest size possible.

Large Square Cut 9½in (24.25cm) squares, cut 3 in GP91BR, GP115BR, GP120BR, GP122MV, PJ38BR and PJ46BR. Total 18 Squares.

Template U Cut 3½in (9cm) wide strips across the width of the fabric. Each strip will give you 11 patches per full width. Cut 12 in BM19OR, BM25MU, GP01BY, GP59GN, GP71OC, GP71PU, GP92BR, GP119RU, 11 in BM08OR, BM13CC, BM15BE, GP20PP, 10 in BM03DR, BM08RD, GP92TM, PJ46BR, 9 in GP71FO. GP91BR, PJ38BR, 8 in BM25SI, GP01GD, 6 in GP115BR, GP120BR and GP122MV. Total 241 Squares.

Template EE Cut 5in (12.75cm) wide strips across the width of the fabric. Each strip will give you 8 patches per full width. Cut 52 in WBS SS.

Binding Cut 8 strips 2½in (6.5cm) across the width of the fabric in GP71TC.

Backing Cut 1 piece 40in x 86in (101.5cm x 218.5cm) and 1 piece 29in x 86in (73.5cm x 218.5cm) in backing fabric.

MAKING THE QUILT
Use a ¼in (6mm) seam allowance throughout and refer to the quilt assembly diagram for fabric placement. Start by piecing the nine-patch blocks, each nine-patch block has 4 squares of one and 5 of another fabric. Following block assembly diagrams a and b make 17 blocks, the finished block is shown in diagram c. Alternating the nine-patch blocks with large squares, piece into 7 rows of 5 blocks. Join the rows to form the quilt centre as shown in the quilt assembly diagram.

MAKING THE BORDERS
Take the template EE squares and piece into 2 borders of 10 squares for the quilt top and bottom and 2 borders of 16 squares for the quilt sides.

BLOCK ASSEMBLY DIAGRAMS

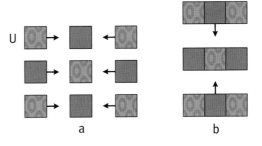

U

a   b   c

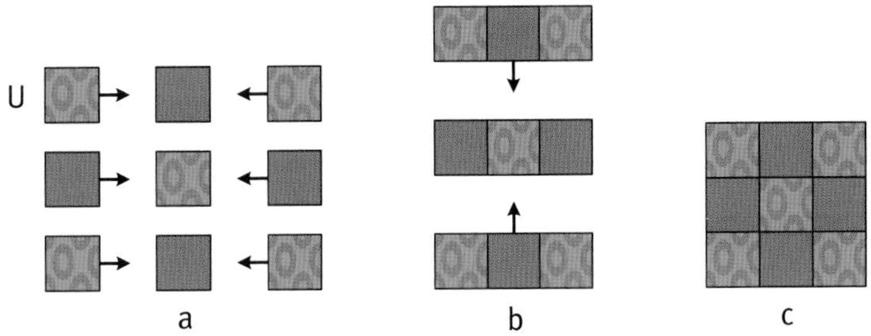

Alternate the stripe direction of the squares throughout making sure the order will run correctly at the corners. Join the borders to the quilt centre, top and bottom first, then sides as shown in the quilt assembly diagram. Take the remaining template U squares and piece into 2 borders of 18 squares for the top

and bottom of the quilt and 2 borders of 26 squares for the quilt sides. Join to the quilt centre as before.

FINISHING THE QUILT
Press the quilt top. Seam the backing pieces using a ¼in (6mm) seam allowance to form a piece approx. 68in

x 86in (173cm x 218.5cm). Layer the quilt top, batting and backing and baste together (see page 140). Using taupe machine quilting tread, free motion quilt in a loose meandering pattern across the surface of the quilt. Trim the quilt edges and attach the binding (see page 141).

QUILT ASSEMBLY DIAGRAM

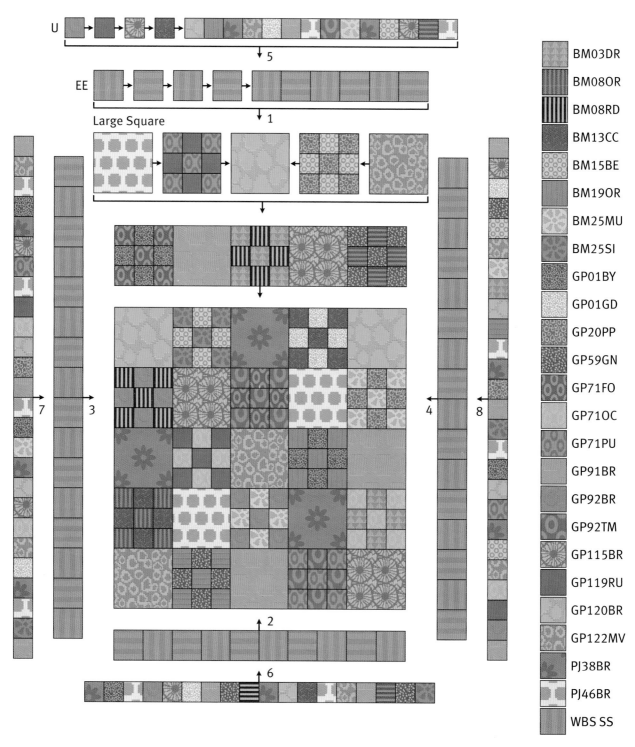

	BM03DR
	BM08OR
	BM08RD
	BM13CC
	BM15BE
	BM19OR
	BM25MU
	BM25SI
	GP01BY
	GP01GD
	GP20PP
	GP59GN
	GP71FO
	GP71OC
	GP71PU
	GP91BR
	GP92BR
	GP92TM
	GP115BR
	GP119RU
	GP120BR
	GP122MV
	PJ38BR
	PJ46BR
	WBS SS

templates

Please refer to the individual instructions for the templates required for each quilt as some templates are used in several projects. The arrows on the templates should be lined up with the straight grain of the fabric, which runs either along the selvedge or at 90 degrees to the selvedge. Following the marked grain lines is important to prevent patches having bias edges along block and quilt edges which can cause distortion. In some quilts the arrows also denote stripe direction.

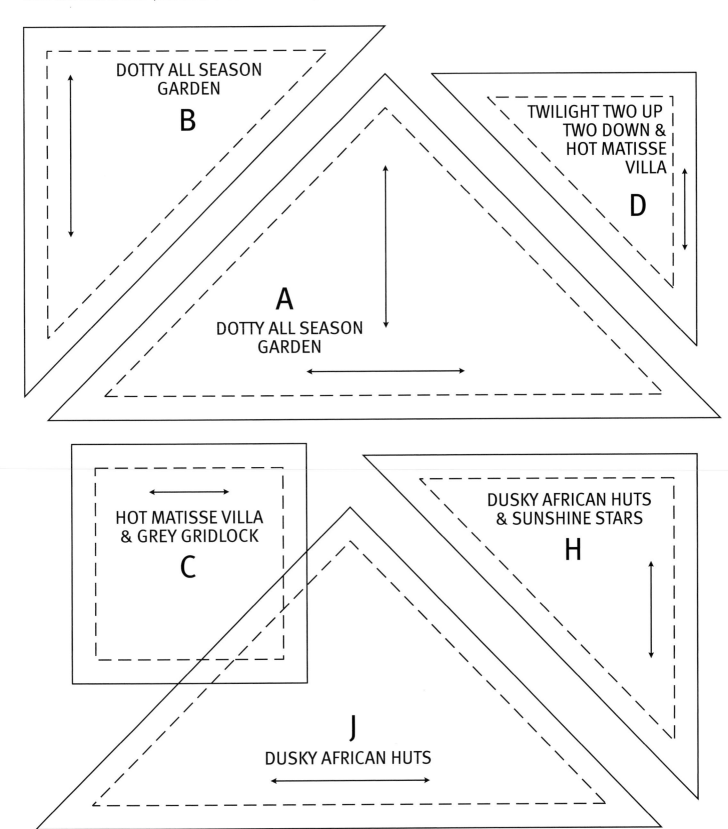

DOTTY ALL SEASON GARDEN B

TWILIGHT TWO UP TWO DOWN & HOT MATISSE VILLA D

DOTTY ALL SEASON GARDEN A

HOT MATISSE VILLA & GREY GRIDLOCK C

DUSKY AFRICAN HUTS & SUNSHINE STARS H

DUSKY AFRICAN HUTS J

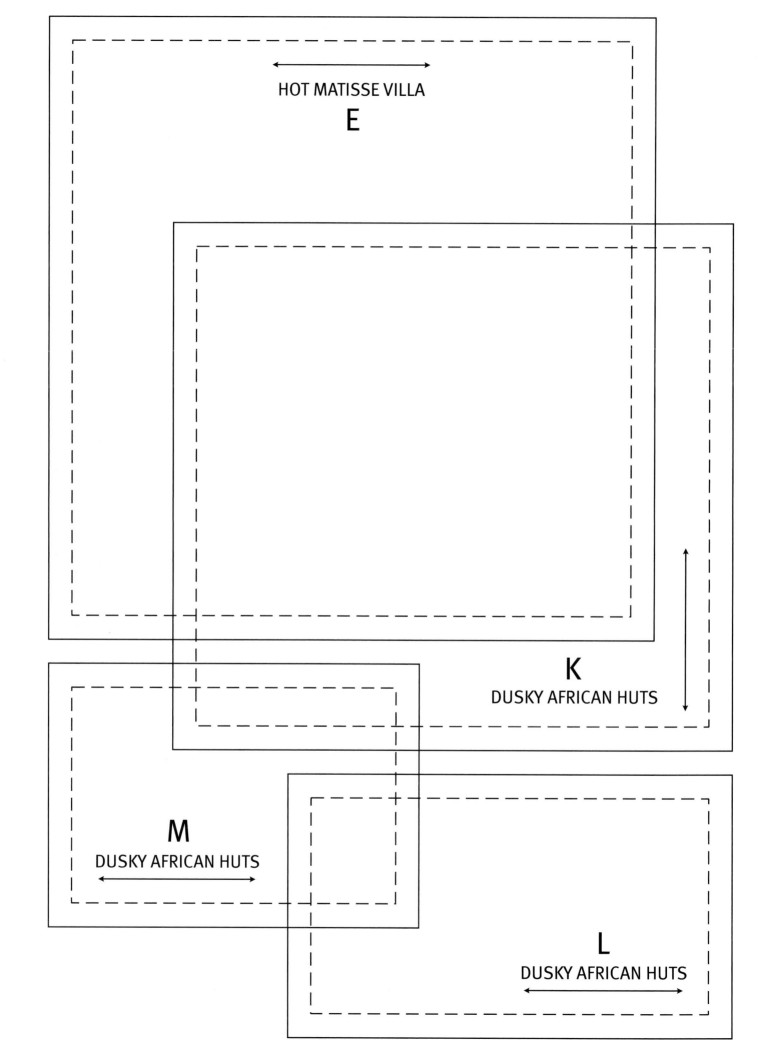

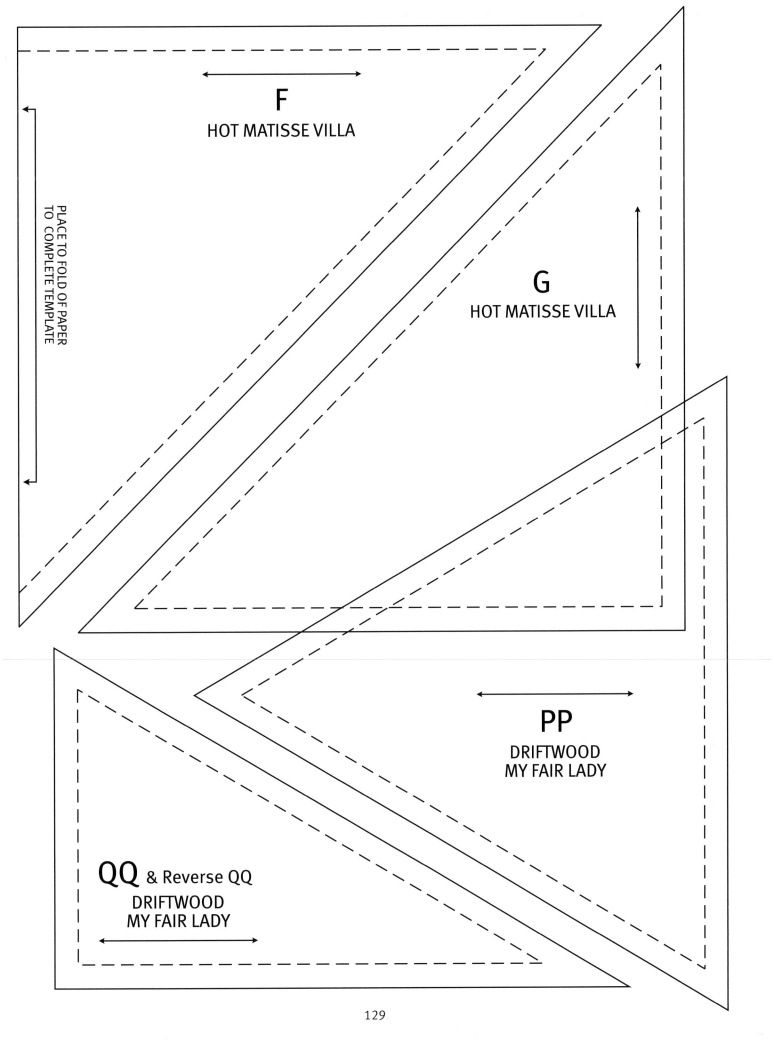

F

HOT MATISSE VILLA

G

HOT MATISSE VILLA

PLACE TO FOLD OF PAPER
TO COMPLETE TEMPLATE

PP

DRIFTWOOD
MY FAIR LADY

QQ & Reverse QQ

DRIFTWOOD
MY FAIR LADY

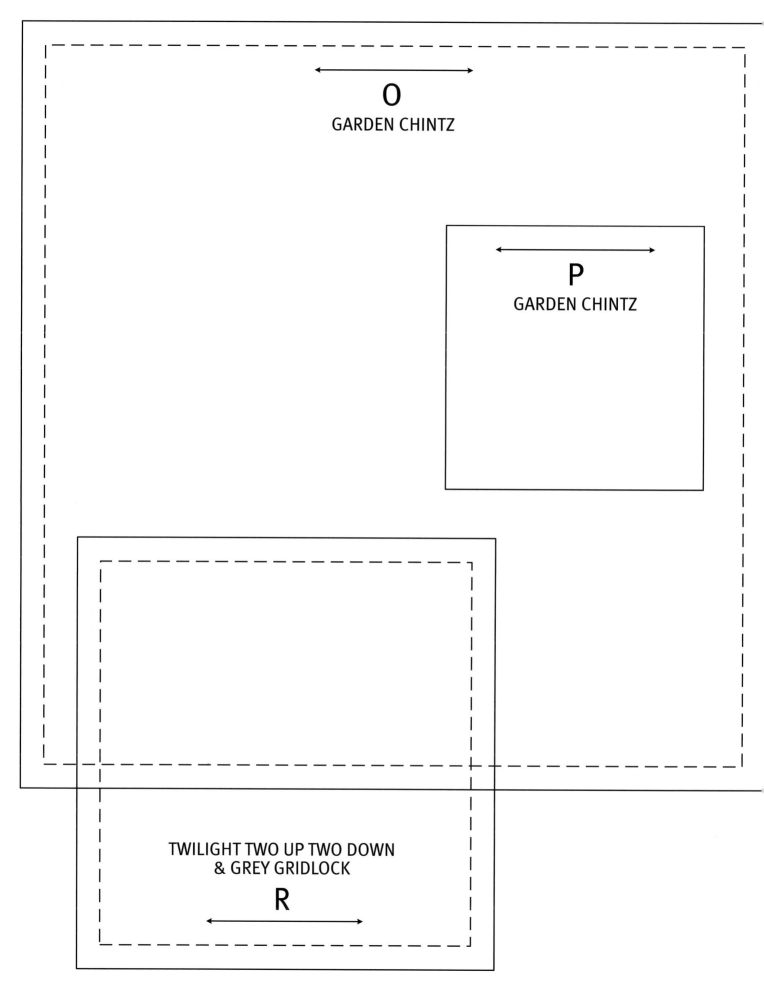

O
GARDEN CHINTZ

P
GARDEN CHINTZ

TWILIGHT TWO UP TWO DOWN
& GREY GRIDLOCK

R

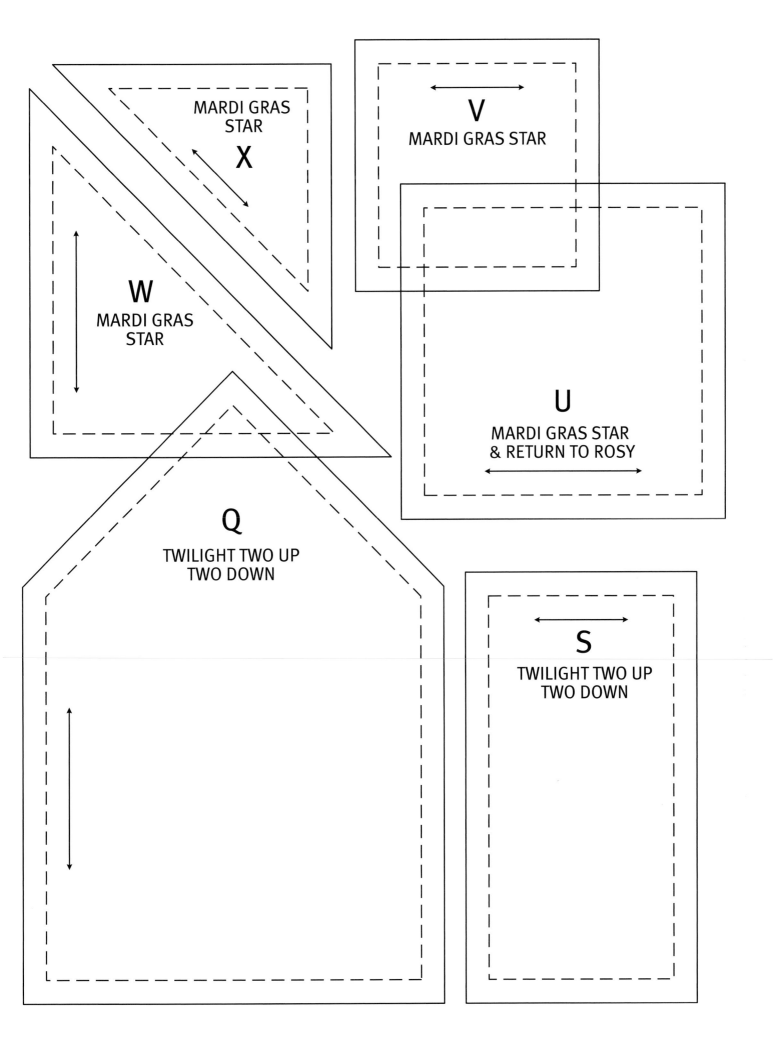

MARDI GRAS
STAR
X

V
MARDI GRAS STAR

W
MARDI GRAS
STAR

U
MARDI GRAS STAR
& RETURN TO ROSY

Q
TWILIGHT TWO UP
TWO DOWN

S
TWILIGHT TWO UP
TWO DOWN

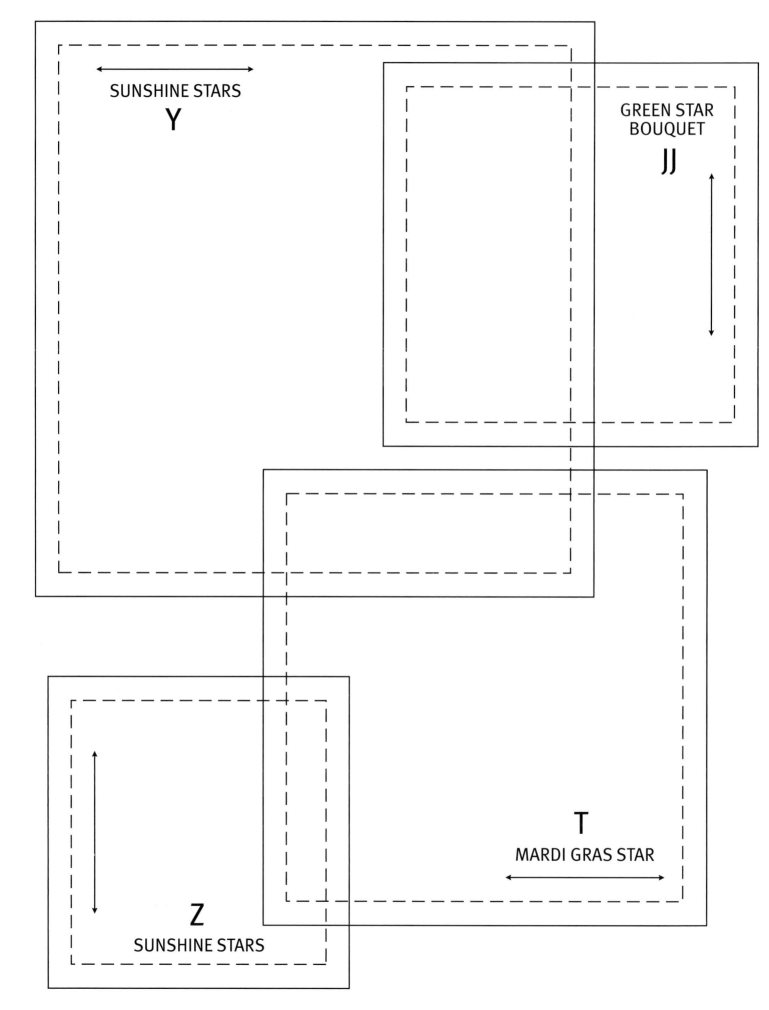

SUNSHINE STARS

Y

GREEN STAR
BOUQUET

JJ

T

MARDI GRAS STAR

Z

SUNSHINE STARS

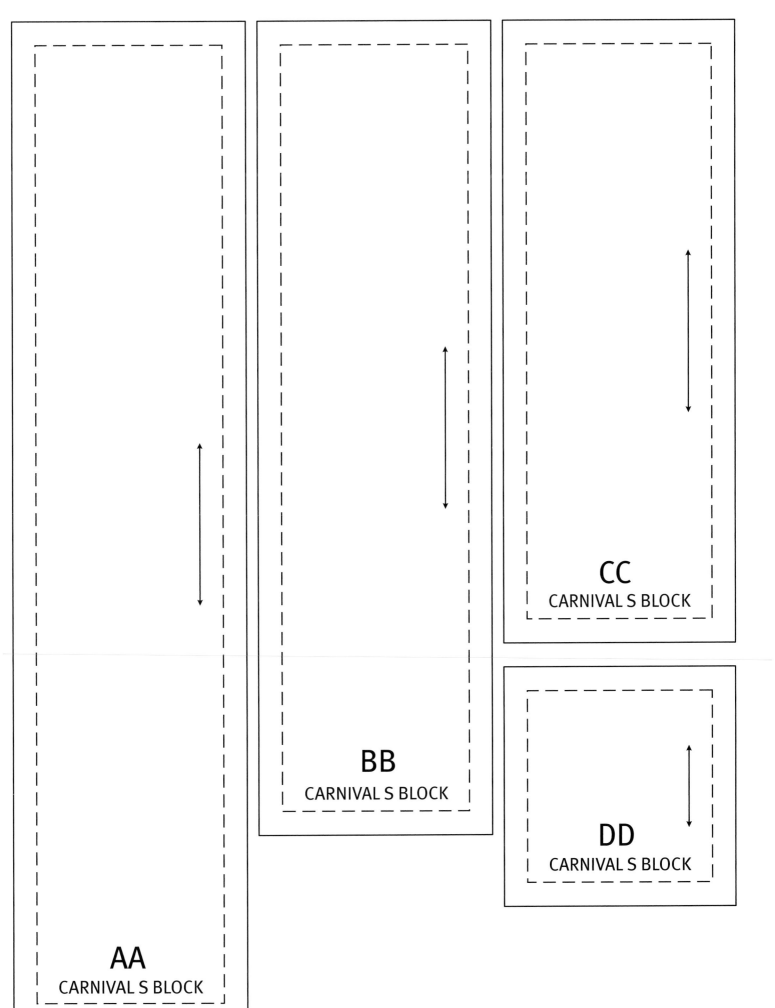

AA
CARNIVAL S BLOCK

BB
CARNIVAL S BLOCK

CC
CARNIVAL S BLOCK

DD
CARNIVAL S BLOCK

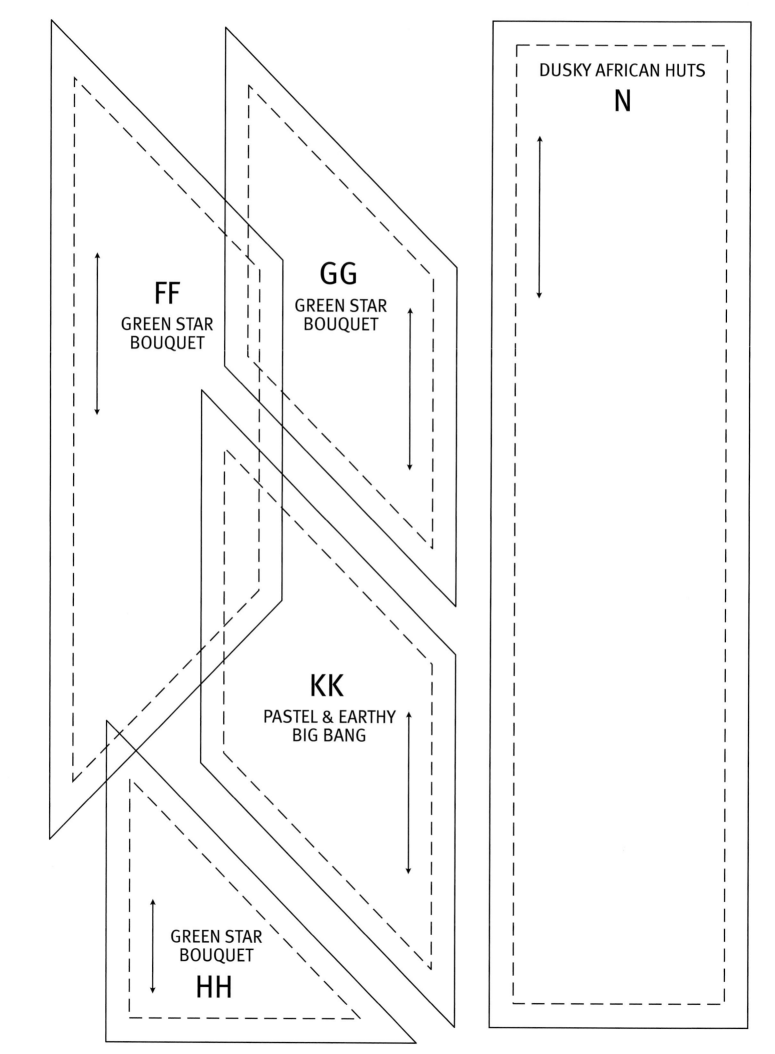

FF
GREEN STAR
BOUQUET

GG
GREEN STAR
BOUQUET

KK
PASTEL & EARTHY
BIG BANG

GREEN STAR
BOUQUET
HH

DUSKY AFRICAN HUTS
N

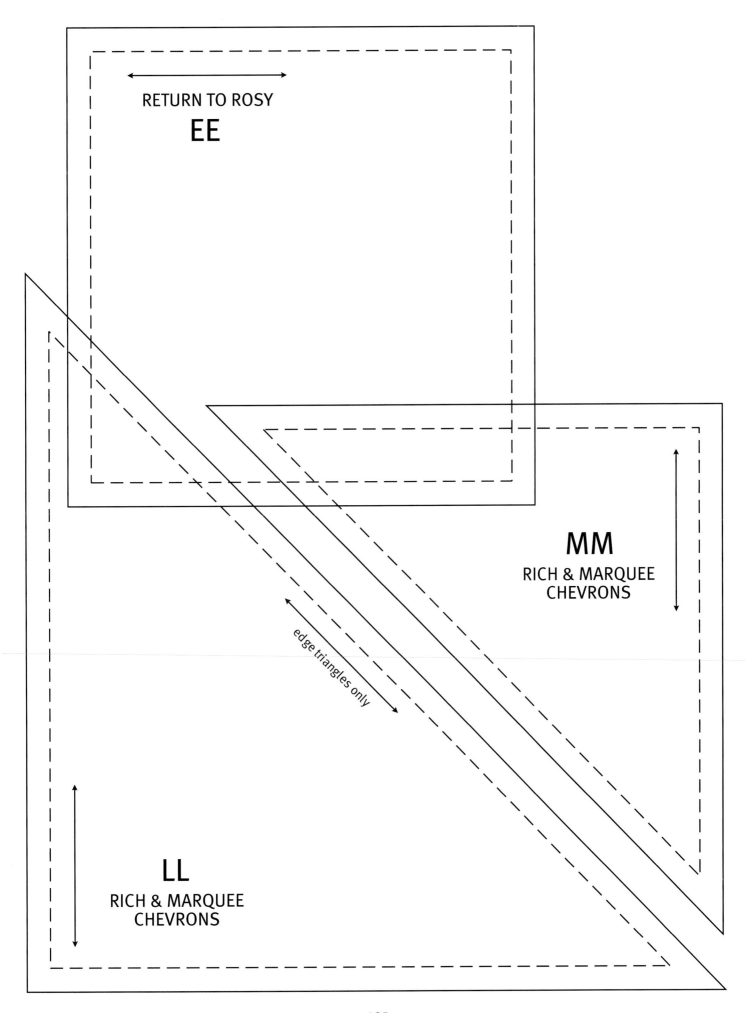

RETURN TO ROSY
EE

MM
RICH & MARQUEE
CHEVRONS

edge triangles only

LL
RICH & MARQUEE
CHEVRONS

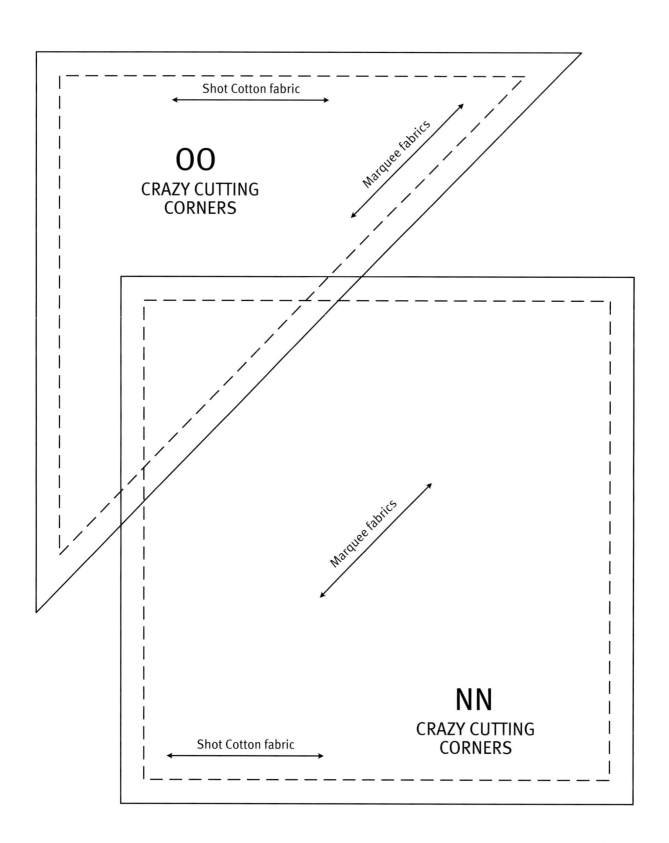

OO
CRAZY CUTTING
CORNERS

Shot Cotton fabric

Marquee fabrics

NN
CRAZY CUTTING
CORNERS

Shot Cotton fabric

Marquee fabrics

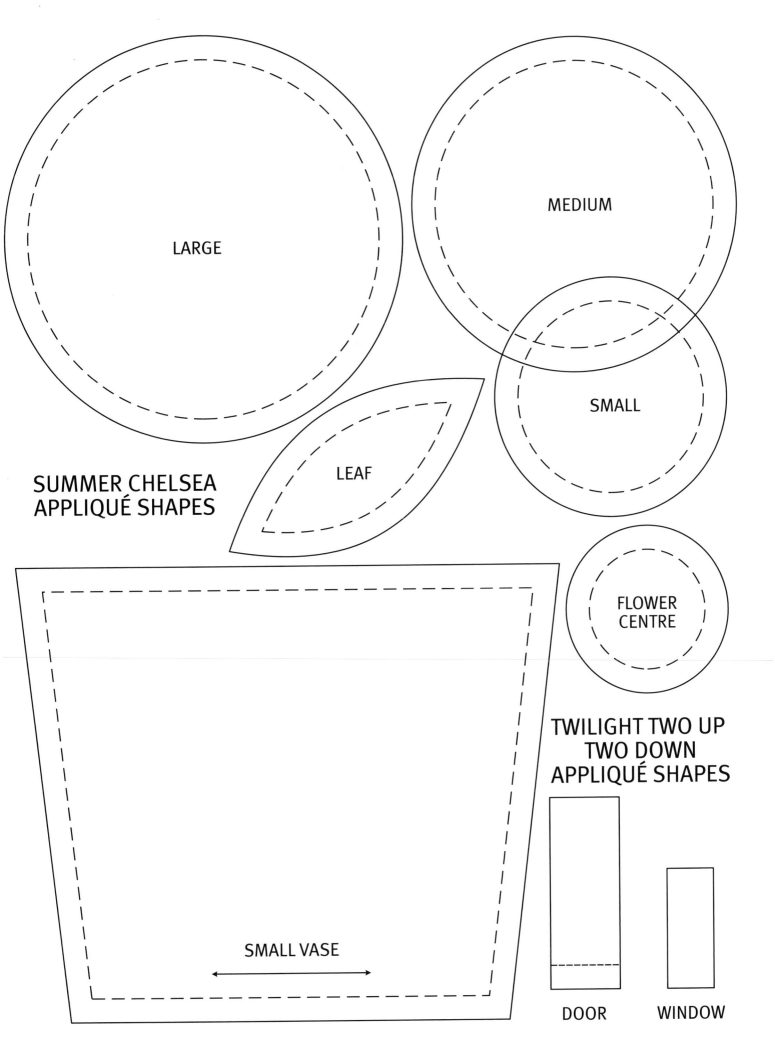

LARGE

MEDIUM

SMALL

LEAF

SUMMER CHELSEA
APPLIQUÉ SHAPES

FLOWER
CENTRE

TWILIGHT TWO UP
TWO DOWN
APPLIQUÉ SHAPES

SMALL VASE

DOOR

WINDOW

patchwork know-how

These instructions are intended for the novice quilt maker. They provide the basic information needed to make the projects in this book. They also include some useful tips.

EXPERIENCE RATINGS
* Easy, straightforward, suitable for a beginner.
** Suitable for the average patchwork and quilter.
*** For the more experienced patchwork and quilter.

ABOUT THE FABRICS
The fabrics used for the quilts in this book are from Kaffe Fassett Collective and carry the relevant fabric codes. The first two letters of the fabric codes denote the designer collection:
GP is the code for the Kaffe Fassett collection
PJ is the code for the Philip Jacobs collection
BM is the code for the Brandon Mably collection.

PREPARING THE FABRIC
Prewash all new fabrics before you begin to ensure that there will be no uneven shrinkage and no bleeding of colours when the finished quilt is laundered. Press the fabric while it is still damp to return crispness to it.
NB All fabric requirements in this book are calculated on a 40in (101.5cm) usable fabric width, to allow for shrinkage and selvedge removal.

MAKING TEMPLATES
Transparent template plastic is the best material to use: it is durable and allows you to see the fabric and select certain motifs. You can also use thin stiff cardboard.

Templates for machine piecing
1 Trace off the actual–sized template provided in this book firstly directly on to template plastic or tracing paper, and then on to thin cardboard. Use a ruler to trace off the straight cutting line, dotted seam line and grain lines.
2 Cut out the traced off template using a craft knife, a ruler and a self–healing cutting mat.
3 Punch holes in the corners of the template, at each point on the seam line, using a hole punch.

Templates for hand piecing
• Make a template as for machine piecing, but do not trace off the cutting line. Use the dotted seam line as the outer edge of the template.

• This template allows you to draw the seam lines directly on to the fabric. The seam allowances can then be cut by eye around the patch.

CUTTING THE FABRIC
With the instructions for each project, there is a summary of all the patch shapes used. Always mark and cut out any border and binding strips first, followed by the largest patch shapes and then the smallest ones, to make the most efficient use of your fabric. The border and binding strips are best cut using a rotary cutter.

Rotary cutting
Rotary cut strips are usually cut across the fabric from selvedge to selvedge, but some projects may vary this rule, so please read through all the instructions before you start cutting the fabrics.

1 Before beginning to cut, press out any folds or creases in the fabric. If you are cutting a large piece of fabric, you will need to fold it several times to fit the cutting mat. When there is only a single fold, place the fold facing you. If the fabric is too wide to be folded only once, fold it concertina-style until it fits your mat. A small rotary cutter with a sharp blade will cut up to six layers of fabric; a large cutter up to eight layers.

2 To ensure that your cut strips are straight and even, the folds must be placed exactly parallel to the straight edges of the fabric and along a line on the cutting mat.

3 Place a plastic ruler over the raw edge of the fabric, overlapping it about ½in (1.25cm). Make sure that the ruler is at right angles to both the straight edges and the fold to ensure that you cut along the straight grain. Press down on the ruler and wheel the cutter away from you along the edge of the ruler.

4 Open out the fabric to check the edge. Don't worry if it's not perfectly straight – a little wiggle will not show when the quilt is stitched together. Re-fold fabric, then place the ruler over the trimmed edge, aligning the edge with the markings on the ruler that match the correct strip width. Cut strip along the edge of the ruler.

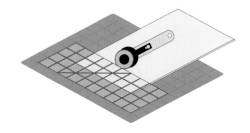

USING TEMPLATES
The most efficient way to cut out templates is by first rotary cutting a strip of fabric to the width stated for your template, and then marking off your templates along the strip, edge to edge at the required angle. This method leaves hardly any waste and gives a random effect to your patches.

A less efficient method is to 'fussy cut' them, where the templates are cut individually by placing them on particular motifs or stripes, to create special effects. Although this method is more wasteful, it yields very interesting results.

1 Place the template face down, on the wrong side of the fabric, with the grain-line arrow following the straight grain of the fabric, if indicated. Be careful though – check with your individual instructions, as some instructions may ask you to cut patches on varying grains.

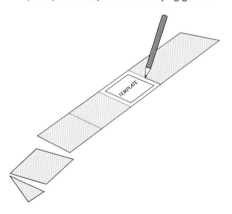

2 Hold the template firmly in place and draw around it with a sharp pencil or crayon, marking in the corner dots or seam lines. To save fabric, position patches close together or even touching. Don't worry if outlines positioned on the straight grain when drawn on striped fabrics do not always match the stripes when cut – this will add a degree of visual excitement to the patchwork!

3 Once you've drawn all the pieces needed, you are ready to cut the fabric, with either a rotary cutter and ruler or a pair of sharp sewing scissors.

BASIC HAND AND MACHINE PIECING
Patches can be stitched together by hand or machine. Machine stitching is quicker, but hand assembly allows you to carry your patches around with you and work on them in every spare moment. The choice is yours. For techniques that are new to you, practise on scrap pieces of fabric until you feel confident.

Machine piecing
Follow the quilt instructions for the order in which to piece the individual patchwork blocks and then assemble the blocks together in rows.

1 Seam lines are not marked on the fabric, so stitch ¼in (6mm) seams using either the machine needle plate, a ¼in (6mm) wide machine foot, or tape stuck to the machine as a guide. Pin two patches with right sides together, matching edges.

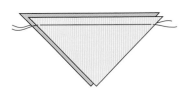

Set your machine at 10–12 stitches per inch (2.5cm) and stitch seams from edge to edge, removing pins as you feed the fabric through the machine.

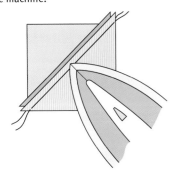

2 Press the seams of each patchwork block to one side before attempting to join it to another block.

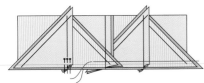

3 When joining rows of blocks, make sure that adjacent seam allowances are pressed in opposite directions to reduce bulk and make matching easier. Pin pieces together directly through the stitch line and to the right and left of the seam. Remove pins as you sew. Continue pressing seams to one side as you work.

Hand piecing
1 Pin two patches with right sides together, so that the marked seam lines are facing outwards.

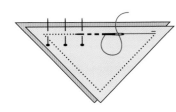

2 Using a single strand of strong thread, secure the corner of a seam line with a couple of back stitches.

3 Sew running stitches along the marked line, working 8–10 stitches per inch (2.5cm) and ending at the opposite seam line corner with a few back stitches. When hand piecing never stitch over the seam allowances.

4 Press the seams to one side, as shown in machine piecing (Step 2).

Inset seams
In some patchwork layouts a patch will have to be sewn into an angled corner formed by the joining of two other patches. Use the following method whether you are machine or hand piecing. Don't be intimidated – this is not hard to do once you have learned a couple of techniques. The seam is sewn from the centre outwards in two halves to ensure that no tucks appear at the centre.

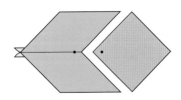

1 Mark with dots exactly where the inset will be joined and mark the seam lines on the wrong side of the fabric on the inset patch.

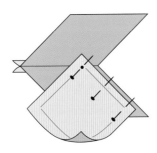

2 With right sides together and inset piece on top, pin through the dots to match the inset points. Pin the rest of the seam at right angles to the stitching line, along one edge of an adjoining patch.

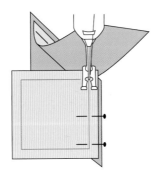

3 Stitch the patch in place along the seam line starting with the needle down through the inset point dots. Secure thread with a backstitch if hand piecing, or stitch forward for a few stitches before backstitching, when machine piecing.

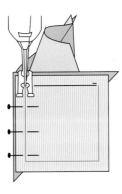

4 Pivot the patch, to enable it to align with the adjacent side of the angled corner, allowing you work on the second half of the seam. Starting with a pin at the inset point once again, pin and stitch the second side in place, as before. Check seams and press carefully.

MACHINE APPLIQUÉ WITH ADHESIVE WEB
To make appliqué very easy you can use adhesive web (which comes attached to a paper backing sheet) to bond the motifs to the background fabric. There are two types of web available: the first keeps the pieces in place while they are stitched, the second permanently attaches the pieces so that no sewing is required. Follow steps 1 and 2 for the non-sew type and steps 1–3 for the type that requires sewing.

1 Trace the reversed appliqué design onto the paper side of the adhesive web leaving a ¼in (6mm) gap between all the shapes. Roughly cut out the motifs ⅛in (3mm) outside your drawn line.

2 Bond the motifs to the reverse of your chosen fabrics. Cut out on the drawn line with very sharp scissors. Remove the backing paper by scoring the centre of the motif carefully with a scissor point and peeling the paper away from the centre out (to prevent damage to the edges). Place the motifs onto the background, noting any which may be layered. Cover with a clean cloth and bond with a hot iron (check instructions for temperature setting as adhesive web can vary depending on the manufacturer).

3 Using a contrasting or toning coloured thread in your machine, work small close zigzag stitches (or a blanket stitch if your machine has one) around the edge of the motifs; the majority of the stitching should sit on the appliqué shape. When stitching up to points stop with the machine needle in the down position, lift the foot of your machine, pivot the work, lower the foot and continue to stitch. Make sure all the raw edges are stitched.

HAND APPLIQUÉ
Good preparation is essential for speedy and accurate hand appliqué. The finger-pressing method is suitable for needle-turning application, used for simple shapes like leaves and flowers. Using a card template is the best method for bold simple motifs such as circles.

Finger–pressing method

1 To make your template, transfer the appliqué design using carbon paper on to stiff card, and cut out the template. Trace around the outline of your appliquéd shape on to the right side of your fabric using a well sharpened pencil. Cut out shapes, adding by eye a ¼in (6mm) seam allowance all around.

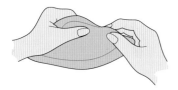

2 Hold shape right side up and fold under the seam, turning along your drawn line, pinch to form a crease. Dampening the fabric makes this very easy. When using shapes with 'points' such as leaves, turn in the seam allowance at the 'point' first, as shown in the diagram. Then continue all round the shape. If your shapes have sharp curves, you can snip the seam allowance to ease the curve. Take care not to stretch the appliqué shapes as you work.

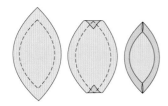

Card template method

1 Cut out appliqué shapes as shown in step 1 of finger-pressing. Make a circular template from thin cardboard, without seam allowances.

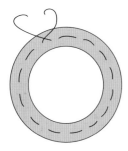

2 Using a matching thread, work a row of running stitches close to the edge of the fabric circle. Place a thin cardboard template in the centre of the fabric circle on the wrong side of the fabric.

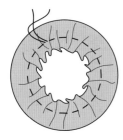

3 Carefully pull up the running stitches to gather up the edge of the fabric circle

around the cardboard template. Press, so that no puckers or tucks appear on the right side. Then, carefully pop out the cardboard template without distorting the fabric shape.

Straight stems

Place fabric face down and simply press over the ¼in (6mm) seam allowance along each edge. You don't need to finish the ends of stems that are layered under other appliqué shapes. Where the end of the stem is visible, simply tuck under the end and finish neatly.

Needle-turning application

Take the appliqué shape and pin in position. Stroke the seam allowance under with the tip of the needle as far as the creased pencil line, and hold securely in place with your thumb. Using a matching thread, bring the needle up from the back of the block into the edge of the shape and proceed to blind-hem in place. (This stitch allows the motifs to appear to be held on invisibly.) To do this, bring the thread out from below through the folded edge of the motif, never on the top. The stitches must be small, even and close together to prevent the seam allowance from unfolding and from frayed edges appearing. Try to avoid pulling the stitches too tight, as this will cause the motifs to pucker up. Work around the whole shape, stroking under each small section before sewing.

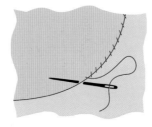

QUILTING

When you have finished piecing your patchwork and added any borders, press it carefully. It is now ready for quilting.

Marking quilting designs and motifs

Many tools are available for marking quilting patterns, check the manufacturer's instructions for use and test on scraps of fabric from your project. Use an acrylic ruler for marking straight lines.

Stencils

Some designs require stencils, these can be made at home, by transferring the designs on to template plastic, or stiff cardboard. The design is then cut away in the form of long dashes, to act as guides for both internal and external lines. These stencils are a quick method for producing an identical set of repeated designs.

Preparing the backing and batting

• Remove the selvedges and piece together the backing fabric to form a backing at least 4in (10cm) larger all round than the patchwork top.

• Choose a fairly thin batting, preferably pure cotton, to give your quilt a flat appearance. If your batting has been rolled up, unroll it and let it rest before cutting it to the same size as the backing.

• For a large quilt it may be necessary to join two pieces of batting to fit. Lay the pieces of batting on a flat surface so that they overlap by around 8in (20cm). Cut a curved line through both layers.

overlap wadding

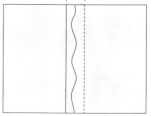

• Carefully peel away the two narrow pieces and discard. Butt the curved cut edges back together. Stitch the two pieces together using a large herringbone stitch.

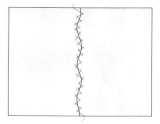

BASTING THE LAYERS TOGETHER

1 On the floor or on a large work surface, lay out the backing with wrong side uppermost. Use weights along the edges to keep it taut.

2 Lay the batting on the backing and smooth it out gently. Next lay the patchwork top, right side up, on top of the batting and smooth gently until there are no wrinkles. Pin at the corners and at the midpoints of each side, close to the edges.

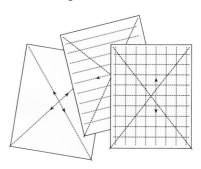

3 Beginning at the centre, baste diagonal lines outwards to the corners, making your stitches about 3in (7.5cm) long. Then, again starting at the centre, baste horizontal and vertical lines out to the edges. Continue basting until you have basted a grid of lines about 4in (10cm) apart over the entire quilt.

4 For speed, when machine quilting, some quilters prefer to baste their quilt sandwich layers together using rust-proof safety pins, spaced at 4in (10cm) intervals over the entire quilt.

HAND QUILTING

This is best done with the quilt mounted on a quilting frame or hoop, but as long as you have basted the quilt well, a frame is not essential. With the quilt top facing upwards, begin at the centre of the quilt and make even running stitches following the design. It is more important to make even stitches on both sides of the quilt than to make small ones. Start and finish your stitching with back stitches and bury the ends of your threads in the batting.

MACHINE QUILTING

• For a flat looking quilt, always use a walking foot on your machine for stitching straight lines, and a darning foot for free–motion quilting.

• It is best to start your quilting at the centre of the quilt and work out towards the borders, doing the straight quilting lines first (stitch-in-the-ditch) followed by the free-motion quilting.

• When free motion-quilting stitch in a loose meandering style as shown in the diagrams. Do not stitch too closely as this will make the quilt feel stiff when finished. If you wish you can include floral themes or follow shapes on the printed fabrics for added interest.

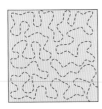

• Make it easier for yourself by handling the quilt properly. Roll up the excess quilt neatly to fit under your sewing machine arm, and use a table or chair to help support the weight of the quilt that hangs down the other side.

FINISHING
Preparing to bind the edges

Once you have quilted or tied your quilt sandwich together, remove all the basting stitches. Then, baste around the outer edge of the quilt ¼in (6mm) from the edge of the top patchwork layer. Trim the back and batting to the edge of the patchwork and straighten the edge of the patchwork if necessary.

Making the binding

1 Cut bias or straight grain strips the width required for your binding, making sure the grain-line is running the correct way on your straight grain strips. Cut enough strips until you have the required length to go around the edge of your quilt.

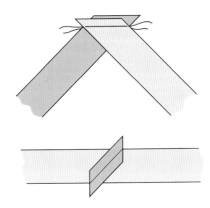

2 To join strips together, the two ends that are to be joined must be cut at a 45 degree angle, as above. Stitch right sides together, trim turnings and press seam open.

Binding the edges

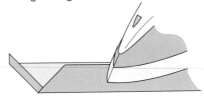

1 Cut the starting end of binding strip at a 45 degree angle, fold a ¼in (6mm) turning to wrong side along cut edge and press in place. With wrong sides together, fold strip in half lengthways, keeping raw edges level, and press.

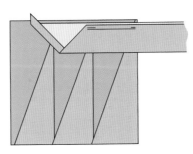

2 Starting at the centre of one of the long edges, place the doubled binding on to the right side of the quilt keeping raw edges level. Stitch the binding in place starting ¼in (6mm)

in from the diagonal folded edge. Reverse stitch to secure, and work ¼in (6mm) in from edge of the quilt towards first corner of quilt. Stop ¼in (6mm) in from corner and work a few reverse stitches.

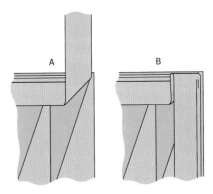

3 Fold the loose end of the binding up, making a 45 degree angle (see A). Keeping the diagonal fold in place, fold the binding back down, aligning the raw edges with the next side of the quilt. Starting at the point where the last stitch ended, stitch down the next side (see B).

4 Continue to stitch the binding in place around all the quilt edges in this way, tucking the finishing end of the binding inside the diagonal starting section.

5 Turn the folded edge of the binding on to the back of the quilt. Hand stitch the folded edge in place just covering binding machine stitches, and folding a mitre at each corner.

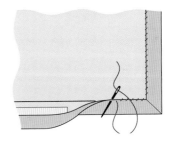

glossary of terms

Adhesive or fusible web This comes attached to a paper backing sheet and is used to bond appliqué motifs to a background fabric. There are 2 types of web available, the first keeps the pieces in place whilst they are stitched, the second permanently attaches the pieces so that no sewing is required.

Appliqué The technique of stitching fabric shapes on to a background to create a design. It can be applied either by hand or machine with a decorative embroidery stitch, such as buttonhole, or satin stitch.

Backing The bottom layer of a quilt sandwich. It is made of fabric pieced to the size of the quilt top with the addition of about 4in (10.25cm) all around to allow for quilting take-up.

Basting or tacking This is a means of holding two fabric layers or the layers of a quilt sandwich together temporarily with large hand stitches, or pins.

Batting or wadding This is the middle layer, or padding in a quilt. It can be made of cotton, wool, silk or synthetic fibres.

Bias The diagonal grain of a fabric. This is the direction which has the most give or stretch, making it ideal for bindings, especially on curved edges.

Binding A narrow strip of fabric used to finish off the edges of quilts or projects; it can be cut on the straight grain of a fabric or on the bias.

Block A single design unit that when stitched together with other blocks create the quilt top. It is most often a square, hexagon, or rectangle, but it can be any shape. It can be pieced or plain.

Border A frame of fabric stitched to the outer edges of the quilt top. Borders can be narrow or wide, pieced or plain. As well as making the quilt larger, they unify the overall design and draw attention to the central area.

Chalk pencils Available in various colours, they are used for marking lines, or spots on fabric.

Cutting mat Designed for use with a rotary cutter, it is made from a special 'self-healing' material that keeps your cutting blade sharp. Cutting mats come in various sizes and are usually marked with a grid to help you line up the edges of fabric and cut out larger pieces.

Design wall Used for laying out fabric patches before sewing. A large wall or folding board covered with flannel fabric or cotton batting in a neutral shade (dull beige or grey work well) will hold fabric in place so that an overall view can be taken of the placement.

Free-motion quilting Curved wavy quilting lines stitched in a random manner. Stitching diagrams are often given for you to follow as a loose guide.

Fussy cutting This is when a template is placed on a particular motif, or stripe, to obtain interesting effects. This method is not as efficient as strip cutting, but yields very interesting results.

Grain The direction in which the threads run in a woven fabric. In a vertical direction it is called the lengthwise grain, which has very little stretch. The horizontal direction, or crosswise grain is slightly stretchy, but diagonally the fabric has a lot of stretch. This grain is called the bias. Wherever possible the grain of a fabric should run in the same direction on a quilt block and borders.

Grain lines These are arrows printed on templates which should be aligned with the fabric grain.

Inset seams or setting-in A patchwork technique whereby one patch (or block) is stitched into a 'V' shape formed by the joining of two other patches (or blocks).

Patch A small shaped piece of fabric used in the making of a patchwork pattern.

Patchwork The technique of stitching small pieces of fabric (patches) together to create a larger piece of fabric, usually forming a design.

Pieced quilt A quilt composed of patches.

Quilting Traditionally done by hand with running stitches, but for speed modern quilts are often stitched by machine. The stitches are sewn through the top, wadding and backing to hold the three layers together. Quilting stitches are usually worked in some form of design, but they can be random.

Quilting hoop Consists of two wooden circular or oval rings with a screw adjuster on the outer ring. It stabilises the quilt layers, helping to create an even tension.

Rotary cutter A sharp circular blade attached to a handle for quick, accurate cutting. It is a device that can be used to cut up to six layers of fabric at one time. It must be used in conjunction with a 'self-healing' cutting mat and a thick plastic ruler.

Rotary ruler A thick, clear plastic ruler printed with lines that are exactly ¼in (6mm) apart. Sometimes they also have diagonal lines printed on, indicating 45 and 60 degree angles. A rotary ruler is used as a guide when cutting out fabric pieces using a rotary cutter.

Sashing A piece or pieced sections of fabric interspaced between blocks.

Sashing posts When blocks have sashing between them the corner squares are known as sashing posts.

Selvedges Also known as selvages, these are the firmly woven edges down each side of a fabric length. Selvedges should be trimmed off before cutting out your fabric, as they are more liable to shrink when the fabric is washed.

Stitch-in-the-ditch or Ditch quilting Also known as quilting-in-the-ditch. The quilting stitches are worked along the actual seam lines, to give a pieced quilt texture.

Template A pattern piece used as a guide for marking and cutting out fabric patches, or marking a quilting, or appliqué design. Usually made from plastic or strong card that can be reused many times. Templates for cutting fabric usually have marked grain lines which should be aligned with the fabric grain.

Threads One hundred percent cotton or cotton-covered polyester is best for hand and machine piecing. Choose a colour that matches your fabric. When sewing different colours and patterns together, choose a medium to light neutral colour, such as grey or ecru. Specialist quilting threads are available for hand and machine quilting.

Walking foot or Quilting foot This is a sewing machine foot with dual feed control. It is very helpful when quilting, as the fabric layers are fed evenly from the top and below, reducing the risk of slippage and puckering.

Yo-Yos A circle of fabric double the size of the finished puff is gathered up into a rosette shape.

ACKNOWLEDGEMENTS
This book was photographed in Dabene near Karlovo in Bulgaria, the home of our friend Chris Mollov. We give a huge thank you to him and his family for their boundless generosity and help when photographing this book and for the memorable meals they cooked for us.

OTHER ROWAN TITLES AVAILABLE
Kaffe Fassett's *Quilt Romance*
Kaffe Fassett's *Quilts en Provence*
Kaffe Fassett's *Quilts in Sweden*

The fabric collection can be viewed online at
www.coatscrafts.co.uk *and* www.westminsterfabrics.com

Rowan 100% cotton premium thread, Anchor embroidery thread, and Prym sewing aids, distributed by
Coats Crafts UK, Green Lane Mill, Holmfirth, West Yorkshire, HD9 2DX.
Tel: +44 (0) 1484 681881 • Fax: +44 (0) 1484 687920

Rowan 100% cotton premium thread and Anchor embroidery thread distributed in the USA by
Westminster Fibers, 3430 Toringdon Way, Charlotte, North Carolina 28277.
Tel: 704 329 5800 • Fax: 704 329 5027

Prym productions distributed in the USA by
Prym-Dritz Corp, 950 Brisack Road, Spartanburg, SC 29303.
Tel: +1 864 576 5050 • Fax: +1 864 587 3353
email: pdmar@teleplex.net

Rowan/Coats Crafts UK, Green Lane Mill, Holmfirth,
West Yorkshire HD9 2DX, England.
Tel: +44 (0) 1484 681881 • Email: ccuk.sales@coats.com
www.coatscrafts.co.uk • www.knitrowan.co.uk

Westminster Lifestyle Fabrics, 3430 Toringdon Way, Suite 301,
Charlotte, NC, U.S.A
Tel: 704-329-5800 • Email: fabric@westminsterfibers.com
www.westminsterfabrics.com

distributors and stockists

Overseas distributors of Rowan fabrics

AUSTRIA
Coats Harlander Ges.m.b.H
Autokaderstraße 29, BT2, 1.OG
1210 Wien
Tel.: 00800 26272800
Email: coats.harlander@coats.com
www.coatscrafts.at

AUSTRALIA
XLN Fabrics
2/21 Binney Road,
Kings Park
New South Wales 2148
Tel: 61-2 -9621-3066
Email: info@xln.co.zu

BENELUX
c/o Coats GmbH
Kaiserstr. 1
79341 Kenzingen
Germany
Tel: +32 (0) 800 77892 (Belgium)
Tel: +31 (0) 800 0226648 (Netherlands)
Tel: +49 (0) 7644 802222 (Luxembourg)
Email: sales.coatsninove@coats.com
www.coatscrafts.be

BRAZIL
Coats Corrente Ltda
Rua Do Manifesto,
705 Ipiranga
Sao Paulo
SP 04209-00
Tel: 5511-3247-8000
www.coatscrafts.br

BULGARIA, GREECE, CYPRUS
Coats Bulgaria EOOD
7 Magnaurska shkola Str.
1784 Sofia, Bulgaria
Tel: +359 2 976 77 72
Email: officebg@coats.com
www.coatsbulgaria.bg (Bulgaria)
www.coatscrafts.gr (Greece)
www.coatscrafts.com.cy (Cyprus)

CZECH REPUBLIC
Coats Czecho s.r.o.
Staré Mesto 246
56932 Staré Mesto
Czech Republic
Tel: 00420 461 616633
Email: galanterie@coats.com
www.coatscrafts.cz

DENMARK
Coats Expotex AB
Box 297
SE-401 24 Goteborg
Tel: +46 31 72145-15
www.coatscrafts.dk

ESTONIA
Coats Eesti As
Ampri tee 9/4 P.K. 2100 Haabneeme
74011 Vlimsi Vald, Harjumaa
Tel: +372 6306 252
www.coatscrafts.co.ee

FINLAND
Coats Opti Crafts Oy
Ketjutie 3
04220 Kerava
Tel: 358-9-274871
www.coatscrafts.fi

FRANCE
Coats France
Division Arts du Fil
c/o Coats GmbH
Kaiserstr. 1
79341 Kenzingen
Germany
Tel: 0810 060002
Email: artsdufil@coats.com
www.coatscrafts.fr

3B COM
7 Rue André Clou
Centre de Gros – Avenue Larrieu
31094 Toulouse Cedex 1
Tel: 33 5 62202096
Email : commercial–3bcom@wanadoo.fr

GERMANY
Coats GmbH
Kaiserstraße 1
79341 Kenzingen
Tel: +49 (0) 7644 802222
Email: kenzingen.vertrieb@coats.com
www.coatsgmbh.de

HUNGARY
Coats Crafts Hungary Kft.
H-7500 Nagyatad
Gyar utca 21
Tel: (36) 12332197
www.coatscrafts.hu

ITALY
Coats Cucirini Srl
Viale Sarca 223
20126 Milano Mi
Tel: +3902 63615210
www.coatscucirini.com

JAPAN
Kiyohara & Co Ltd
4-5-2 Minamikyuhoji-Machi
Chuo-Ku
Osaka
541-8506
Tel: 81 6 6251 7179

KOREA
Coats Korea Co Ltd
5F Kuckdong B/D
935-40 Bangbae-Dong
Seocho-Gu, Seoul
South Korea
Tel: 82-2-521-6262

LATVIA
Coats Latvija SIA
Mükusalas iela 41 b
Rïga LV-1004
Tel: +371 67625031
Email: info@coats.lv
www.coatscrafts.lv

LITHUANIA
Coats Lietuva UAB
A.Juozapavicaus g. 6/2,
LT-09310 Vilinius
Tel: 3705- 2730972
www.coatscrafts.lt

NEW ZEALAND
Fabco Limited
280 School Road
P.O. Box 84-002
Westgate
Auckland 1250
Tel: 64-9-411-9996
Email: info@fabco.co.nz

NORWAY
Coats Expotex AB
Box 297
SE-401 24 Goteborg
Tel: +46 31 7214515
www.coatscrafts.no

POLAND
Coats Polska Sp.z.o.o
ul. Kaczencowa 16
91-214 Lodz
Tel: 48 42 254 0400
www.coatscrafts.pl

PORTUGAL
Companhia de Linha Coats & Clark, SA
Quinta de Cravel
4430-968 Vila Nova de Gaia
Tel: 00 351-223 770 700

SINGAPORE
Quilts and Calicos
163 Tanglin Road
03-13 Tanglin Mall
247933
Tel: 00 65-688 74708

SLOVAK REPUBLIC
Coats s.r.o.
Kopcianska 94
85101 Bratislava
Tel: 00421 2 6820 1061
Email: galanteria@coats.com
www.coatscrafts.sk

SOUTH AFRICA
Arthur Bales PTY Ltd
62 4th Avenue
PO Box 44644
Linden 2104
Tel: 27-11-888-2401

SPAIN
Coats Fabra, S.A.
Sant Adria, 20
E-08030 Barcelona
Tel: 00 +34 93-290 84 00
www.coatscrafts.es

SWITZERLAND
Coats Stroppel AG
Stroppelstrasse 20
5417 Untersiggenthal
Tel: 00800 26272800
Email: coats.stroppel@coats.com
www.coatscrafts.ch

SWEDEN
Coats Expotex AB
Box 297
SE-401 24 Goteborg
Tel: +46 31 7214515
www.coatscrafts.se

TAIWAN
Long Teh Trading Co
No. 71 Hebei W. St.
Taichung City
Tel: 886-4-225-6698

TURKEY
Coats
Kavacik Mah
Ekinciler Cad
Mecip Fazil SK. No. 8
Istanbul
Tel: +90 216 425 8810
www.coatsturkiye.com.tr

UK
Rowan/Coats Crafts UK
Green Lane Mill
Holmfirth
West Yorkshire
HD9 2DX
Tel: 01484 681881
Email: ccuk.sales@coats.com
www.coatscrafts.co.uk

U.S.A/Canada
Westminster Lifestyle Fabrics
3430 Toringdon Way
Suite 301
Charlotte
NC
Tel: 704-329-5800
Email: fabric@westminsterfibers.com
www.westminsterfabrics.com